Walking in Your Shoes to Restore The American Dream

Joe Sestak
with Jake Sternberger

INFINITY
PUBLISHING

ISBN 978-1-4958-0559-2
ISBN 978-1-4958-0560-8 eBook
Library of Congress Catalog Card Number: 0000-0000

Published March 2015

INFINITY PUBLISHING
1094 New DeHaven Street, Suite 100
West Conshohocken, PA 19428-2713
Toll-free (877) BUY BOOK
Local Phone (610) 941-9999
Fax (610) 941-9959
Info@buybooksontheweb.com
www.buybooksontheweb.com

To the love of my entire life, my lovely wife, Susan. When you entered it, I thought I could never be happier...until you gave us Alex. Where would we be without our beautiful daughter, as she puts her arms around us and says, "Come here you two." Talk about love – I live it with both of you every day, and thank all above for it on every day.

CONTENTS

Section III
Restoring Our Workforce – All Hands on Deck

Section IV
Restoring Our Promises – I've Got Your Six

Section V
Restoring Our Future – Full Steam Ahead

PROLOGUE

❦

Today, the biggest deficit in America is the trust deficit. This deficit is not because Americans don't trust each other, but because they have a fundamental distrust of America's leaders – and for good reason. Too often it is the case that our government leaders want to be judged by *what they say* and *how well they say it* instead of *what they do* and *how well they do it*. Worse yet, they do not want to be accountable for what they say they are going to do.

This book is not an autobiography. It is not a tell-all. It was not written with an eye toward what is politically acceptable to say. This book is about restoring the American Dream, the steps we must take to do that, and it is the vehicle through which you can hold me accountable.

After 31 years in the Navy, four years serving my constituents as a Congressman, and three years teaching in Pennsylvania's colleges and universities, there are two major things I came to appreciate. The first is that very much like Scout said in *To Kill a Mockingbird*, "You never really know a man until you stand in his shoes and walk around in them." Understanding the viewpoints of those you serve and how policy decisions affect them requires more than just empathy – it requires walking in their shoes. This is just what I did; I walked 422 miles across Pennsylvania, from the New Jersey border to Ohio's, walking in the shoes of different groups of Pennsylvanians

I met along the way, from laborers to students, the poor to business owners, and veterans and seniors.

The second thing I came to believe is that there are truly two core tenets of the American character: rugged individualism and the common enterprise. To put the Dream back in reach for Americans, we must balance those two core tenets in harmony such that each individual has the opportunity to be all they can be, but never measuring their achievement apart from our shared enterprise as a nation because we are all in this together. Throughout our history, the leaders that best blended these two tenets in their policies accomplished the most in making the Dream a reality – but they did it by being willing to be held accountable for the results.

Nothing less than the future of the country is at stake. If the American Dream is not restored, America will lose what makes our nation great. That is why, now more than ever, we need leaders willing to mend the trust deficit through personal accountability for their actions – putting the Dream back within reach for all Americans.

Joe Sestak

15 February, 2015

ACKNOWLEDGMENTS

M y Mom and my Dad – Kathleen Sestak and Captain Joseph Sestak – are who I aspire to be, and I thank you every day for your endless love and matchless personal example of how to be. And my sisters – Kathy, Barbara, Ann, Elizabeth, Margaret and Pat – are also of boundless love and support, making real the word "family." My brother, Richard who, even in the heavens remains the ballast of my ship, I miss you so much. I love you all.

I deeply thank the sailors I worked with, lived with and went to war with over my 31 years in the Navy – they truly are our national treasure. And my deepest of appreciation to all those I met and served as a Congressman over four wonderful years. Both groups of Americans permitted me to experience and understand Scout's words in *To Kill a Mockingbird*, "You never really know a man until you stand in his shoes and walk around in them." I learned and experienced through them all the challenges we have as individuals and as families, and how best we can come together to resolve them, as we also serve our nation.

To the students at Pennsylvania's outstanding institutions of learning – Carnegie Mellon University, Dickinson College, Cheyney University, the United States Army War College and Penn State University Dickinson School of Law and School of International Affairs – I thank you for your creativity and resourceful insights as you helped me over the past few years in our courses together as your professor to better understand the policies that can restore the American Dream for those whose shoes I have walked in.

I thank Anka Lee for his unmatched help in better appreciating our approach to issues overseas that today so immediately impact us here at home, and how best to address them.

And to Jake Sternberger to whom I owe this book for accepting the daunting task of helping to present what America needs to be all it must be. Incomparable, no one did more to bring this all about, nor is there anyone better to have alongside me in the journey to produce it. A consummate professional, from his writing to his innovative ideas and from a readiness to challenge established thought to a friendship I value more than anything, I owe this day to him.

I would be lost at sea adrift, however, if it were not for the love of my life, my wife, Susan. I owe her my life, for she creates it for me every day. I cannot wait until I wake up and see her every day, and I cannot fathom a moment without you, Susan. Thank you for your love, eternally. And thank you even more for the light of our lives, Alex. Precious, loving, strong, our joyous essence, she penned the words above her painting of a pair of shoes, "Joe Sestak is Walking in your Shoes." She more than anyone taught me about life – and I love you even more than life, Alex.

Section I

RESTORING THE DREAM

Chapter 1

Rugged Individualism, the Common Enterprise, and Accountable Leadership

A Sailor in Politics

Over the last several decades, it has become popular for public officials to force a pitched philosophical battle upon the American people. Their rhetoric separates Americans from Americans, pits "the 99 percent" against "the 1 percent," divides "true believers" from those who "believe differently," classifies Americans as either "makers" or "takers", and presents our people with a Hobson's choice of either ending government service to our citizens or using government to solve everything.

As the divisive rhetoric escalated, our people continued to endure declining economic mobility and stagnant wages – two troublesome developments that featured prominent in many campaign messages, though most merely focused on blame instead of offering ideas needed to address these challenges facing our country. This is a failure of leadership – an assault on American unity at the expense of the American family. As a result of this failure, almost four-fifths[1] of Americans no longer believe in the American Dream – the idea that our children, based on their efforts, will have the opportunity to do better than we have done.

At this critical stage in our nation's history, divisive rhetoric is not what we need from our leaders. Americans yearn for a new type of leadership – focused, purposeful, and responsible people in public service who are willing to be held accountable for the actions needed to guide our ship of state through rough seas. We need leaders who will help us restore the American Dream, and can give our nation a sense of direction – and achievable benchmarks – as we strive to get there.

During my 31-year career as a leader in the United States Navy, I saw how American leadership is most effective when it embraces the dual tenets of our unique national character: rugged individualism in pursuit of the common mission. Our sailors were each provided the individual opportunity to be all they could be, while valuing having one another's back because they recognized "they were in it together" in accomplishing their common purpose. It is an approach that brings unity to a mission, not divisiveness. To ensure their individual achievement, we provided every sailor career-long training and education, enabling each of them to contribute fully to our general overall military readiness. And we retained our sailors' commitment because each had the opportunity to achieve individually the skills he or she valued as their personal contribution. We created ladders of opportunity and our people were brave enough to climb them on their own.

Of equal priority is the requirement that those in charge must hold themselves accountable for results – good or bad. If a ship runs aground, even if it is by the fault of other crew members, the captain in command of the ship is rightly held accountable for mistakes within his command. Accountability means answering for oneself; taking responsibility for one's deeds, not one's intentions. In government today, too few leaders are – or are willing to be – held accountable for their actions.

Accountable leadership gets results and changes cultures because it earns the trust of people who then want to follow. The military's experience offers a fine example. When I entered the Navy in the midst of the Vietnam War, the military ranked last among our national institutions in the public trust. When I retired over three decades later, it ranked first. This wasn't just outside changes in geopolitics or the way we deployed our military; rather, it was the changes we made ourselves in the way we assessed plans and measured benchmarks, conducted rigorous oversight, and demanded strict accountability – from our leadership. On this front, the military did an admirable job in the last generation to regain the public's trust by ensuring that every member of the services – from the most senior flag officer to the most newly enlisted sailor, soldier, marine, airman, or guardsman – is held accountable for his or her actions.

The same, unfortunately, cannot be said of our political leadership today. After I left the Navy, I went on to serve in Congress and saw that, on the whole, our elected leaders were failing to hold themselves accountable. And that's why today it is Congress that ranks last among our national institutions in the public's trust.

In Congress, I witnessed firsthand what the American people have already been feeling innately. I watched "shocked" congressmen chide corporate executives for using tax avoidance techniques, while disregarding that it is *Congress* who writes the codes that so many companies use to avoid taxes. I heard legislators lament about oversight agencies stacked with industry insiders who write rules allowing corporations to fill out their own inspection reports, while failing to acknowledge that the agencies' rulemaking authority comes from legislation that *Congress* writes. Too few of our elected officials are willing to hold themselves accountable for the diminishing American Dream.

One particular night in 2008 stood out as a stark illustration of this glaring lack of accountability in Congress. We were home in our congressional districts during a short recess when President George W. Bush's Treasury Secretary, Hank Paulson, asked to speak with the majority party's House members. Lehman Brothers had failed, and there was a growing fear that a perilous situation was developing on Wall Street. In listening to Paulson on the conference call, the assembled Democrats could hear the timber in his voice as he soberly said that if "we" did not act within the next two weeks, America would face an economic collapse as brutal as the Great Depression.

Immediately upon returning to Washington, the members of the Democratic Congressional Caucus met in a closed meeting to be briefed on the broad outlines of the President's proposed Troubled Asset Relief Program (TARP) to rescue Wall Street and America's economy. I listened in amazement as the first few members stood up to speak and largely said, "Don't touch it, *they* caused it, *they* should have to take the blame, and we shouldn't be held accountable for trying to fix it." To me, a simple sailor, the American ship of state had been hit by a torpedo, and instead of worrying about how best to caulk the resulting hole in the hull to salvage the economy and save the crew, members were focusing on their own political safety and avoiding any responsibility – and by extension, any accountability for their actions.

Eventually, there was one senior Congressman who stood up and, using language I recognized from my Navy days, got everyone to stop the partisan plotting and at least listen about working with the other side to save the country from further devastation. It was a stark contrast: accountability for the people's well-being versus the fear of losing the next election – saving the ship versus saving oneself.

Then, after the House voted on the bill (which failed, although it was later passed as the nation's banks refused to lend without the assurance of the bill), I found myself going on television a dozen times the next day to explain what exactly the bill had aimed to do to save the economy from collapse. To my surprise, I didn't have to fight other members for airtime. In fact, I was called back repeatedly because in the midst of the uncertainty about accountability, nobody else wanted to go on to be either associated with or against the bill.

In my time traveling across the Commonwealth of Pennsylvania, I found that people wanted leaders who will figure out what is best for the country based on facts and analysis, plot a course of action, and be held accountable for the results. On the whole, Americans don't care if we go left or right around an obstacle, they just want us to do it well. The people are not debating about big government versus small government; they just want an effective government. They want a government that gives them the opportunity to apply their innate ability, intellect, ambition, and persistence for their individual achievement, while ensuring a shared investment from our collective resources so that we all might benefit.

In short, what I have found is that the American character is based on the same things I saw promoted most rigorously in the Navy and, sadly, so widely written off in Congress – an understanding and an embrace of the alliance between rugged individualism and the common enterprise – the idea that by securing fair *individual* opportunities for all, we could pursue and safeguard the commonwealth of *our* county together. And the people want to have a government that balances both through accountable leadership.

A Sailor with a Sextant

After I left Congress in 2011, I began teaching the young people of Pennsylvania as a college professor, where I had the time to reflect more deeply on this concept of effective government based on pursuing a fine balance between rugged individualism and the common purpose. In my research as well as conversations with many Pennsylvanians throughout the state, I found myself constantly referring back to the Constitution. Each time, I was struck by how the Preamble so perfectly encapsulated our national endeavor. "We the people" embodies two concepts – that it is *the people*, each a rugged individual, with his or her own talents, inventiveness, and goals, who together make up our shared common enterprise so that *we* may be the shining city upon the hill. Never before had a government been constituted on the idea that the good of the country ("a more perfect union") is based on individual opportunity ("the blessings of liberty") and shared enterprise ("the general welfare").

These twin constitutional pillars were not mere philosophy, but a practical pathway for governing. Right after the Constitution was put into effect in 1789, one of the first acts of Congress was to reenact the Northwest Ordinance, which originated under the less-than-perfect Articles of Confederation. George Washington signed Congress's new ordinance because it encouraged rugged individuals to move forward with their families into the western frontier, promising that in each territory public schools would be built to educate the children of settlers. This guarantee of schooling for the next generation signaled that settling the west wouldn't mean you were entirely on your own, but that *together* we would ensure a better opportunity for the even braver ventures of our children – and we would do it with a citizenry educated enough to protect the fundamental freedoms for which the original thirteen colonies had fought. These hardy frontiersmen had the opportunity as rugged individuals to provide their families a bright, thriving livelihood while the nation's common enterprise benefited enormously by western settlements delivering the needed growth in the national economic muscle and geographic security.

For much the same reason that the new American government directed that education be made available for westward settlers, the new Congress also felt it prudent to establish a mandatory health care system for American merchant sailors – not because our first Congress was full of liberals, but because, by practical recognition, they understood that much of our new maritime nation's economic enterprise was wholly reliant upon a robust merchant fleet manned by a healthy, productive crew. It's the same reason why today our nation provides for the common healthcare of our military members and their families, not because of any liberal bent but because of the pragmatic dividends that our country benefits from a healthy, ready warrior force – and one we can retain.

The founders knew that if the American Experiment was going to work, government needed to provide a fair individual opportunity for our shared prosperity, an alliance of rugged individualism and the common enterprise. And yet, this philosophical foundation of the American Dream was not born overnight – it took centuries to develop in Europe from those opposed to the monarchies. When the Constitution was being written, our forefathers drew their inspiration from the evolution of 200 years of Enlightenment philosophy and the Protestant reformation, both oriented around the defense of individual liberty against the injustices of authoritative power. When English kings decided to spend treasure on royal extravagancies, they arbitrarily raised revenues on subjects in the name of security and order. When faraway archbishops decided that their cathedrals needed gilding, they tithed the common villagers in exchange for the promise of eternal salvation. For good reason, centralized power was seen as the very enemy of freedom.

Against this power and in the name of rugged individualism, America's first colonists set out across an ocean to establish self-government. In defense of self-government's newfound liberties, their descendants rebelled from the Crown. To ensure their posterity would remain free from coercive power, they wrote a Constitution establishing a limited government. And to make sure that individual liberties would not be infringed, The Bill of Rights was added.

Because of a centuries-old European history of governmental abuse, the harm from a government that could intrude upon individual rights was always foremost in our founders' minds. Our Constitution makes clear what government *cannot* do with regard to our individual freedoms, such as interfering with our liberties in speech, religion, and the press. But our founders also understood that government, when properly balanced and checked, could also be capable of positively *advancing the liberties* of its citizens. So even as our early American statesmen worked hard to defend against coercive authority, they wisely devised a system of *democratic,* pragmatic government to safeguard individual rights while enhancing the general welfare. What is not proscribed, "We the People" can prescribe.

As our nation developed, we remained faithful to the conviction that a government "of, for, and by the people" could still protect and advance the people's individual freedoms – even as commerce, business, and financing interests concentrated the power of the private market as they strove to meet the economic needs of the time. This use of government's power was not in competition with private corporate power. Rather, it was supportive of the goals of both the private market and the people. When Wall Street refused to invest in the transcontinental railroad, President Lincoln pushed for "We the People" – through government – to build it ourselves because he saw the benefit in joining our two coasts for commerce while at the same time allowing men and women to chart their individual opportunity in the territories in between. Similarly, when he saw that more than just the guarantee of public schooling was needed, Lincoln established land-grant universities focusing on science and engineering to ensure our industrial capabilities could compete with Europe while at the same time providing individual citizens with greater educational and training opportunities to be all they might be.

As the country changed to keep up with the industrial revolution, a new yoke of private corporate power grew too powerful and, in response, the government "of the people" worked (albeit imperfectly) to protect and advance consumers' and workers' individual liberties without tearing down whole sectors of the economy. In fact, these activities sponsored *greater* productivity. For example, President Theodore Roosevelt created the Food and Drug Administration to protect the people against the growing number of tragic deaths caused by poisonous products sold by unconcerned manufacturers. But as consumer confidence in products grew, so did sales. Similarly, President Taft created the Department of Labor to ensure freedom from unsafe working conditions in dangerous factories. And as workers became safer, productivity soared.

In the shadow of the Great Depression, President Franklin Roosevelt outlined in his "Economic Bill of Rights" the liberties that would be assured *by* government's power: the "freedom from want" for health care, housing, clothing, jobs, social security, and education, acknowledging that "necessitous men are not free men." In doing so, Roosevelt was continuing the tradition begun by our founders and best summarized by President Lincoln, who described the Civil War as "a struggle for maintaining in the world that form and substance of government whose leading object is to elevate the condition of men – to lift the artificial weights from all shoulders – to clear the paths of laudable pursuit for all, to afford an unfettered start, and a fair chance, in the race of life."

Based on our country's foundation in the Bill of Rights, the practical application of the desires of "We the People," and the capacity to use our government to help expand liberties to achieve the individual's – and our common – enterprise, the American Dream remained alive and well. Keeping with this foundation, President Dwight Eisenhower created the Interstate Highway System because he recognized that our shared mobility meant greater personal freedom and enhanced commerce as business' products flowed to every corner of our nation. Eisenhower passed the National Defense Student Loan program because he knew that if we were to be competitive with the Soviet Union, we needed men and women who could create the technology to take us into the heavens and into foreign markets with desired products. Shared opportunity was shared prosperity, and common wealth was common strength.

Through balancing rugged individualism and the common enterprise, government became a force of accountability for the achievement of the American Dream; the right of the people, as the Declaration of Independence proclaimed, to create a government "most likely to effect their Safety and Happiness." Once given the tools and the opportunity to do so, millions of Americans moved into the middle class and, as they pursued their individual happiness, were empowered to contribute their fullest to our national welfare. Small businesses became the engine of our economy and our sources of innovation. We became a country of tall ladders that we built together for all those brave and dedicated enough to climb them on their own. All we asked of those who climbed was to help add more rungs for our children to climb even higher, because though we are rugged individuals, no one achieves the American Dream alone.

This is our true American Exceptionalism, our creation of an unparalleled environment for individual opportunity by both the establishment of individual rights and our shared investment of our collective resources; by a people striving for their own rugged individualism, but never measuring it apart from the common enterprise. The American Dream grew out of these two great values of our American character that took root simultaneously, individual strengths sharpened by a shared alliance, perpetually brokered by a representative government that constantly pushed and fought to expand that benefit to more and more people who were once excluded. Our government was crafted to protect people's liberties from its power, even as that government's power is used, judiciously and purposefully, to advance those liberties – particularly equality of opportunity, even when challenged by private power – for the betterment of America.

And yet somehow, our leaders today have completely lost track of that balance. Instead of continued American progress, our lexicon has swelled with shorthand phrases that have come, over time, to define our time: Enron, WMD, Katrina, fiscal cliff, Super-committee, Bernie Madoff, AIG, filibuster, red and blue, I win...you lose. Not to mention a steady procession of elected officials and civic leaders who have violated the public trust.

Today, it is clear that unaccountable power has harmed our individual liberties and therefore our advancement as a nation. It's not just *government power* infringing our freedoms, it's also *powerful interests* that fight an individual's access to government, to information, to the ballot box, to a better life based on fair return for labor – while maintaining their own power, particularly in the form of moneyed admittance to government officials. Some private power even structures its profits so that our taxes are used to subsidize their employees or their overseas business expenses. And it's our leaders who lack the courage and accountability to stand up against the harms of power to the American Dream, as they fear it can mean losing their own job.

Today's understandable lack of faith in our government and its leaders has ravaged not only our democratic process, but ultimately undermines our sense of national unity – what we stand for and what we are capable of. It is not just politics. The public trust has been devastated by fraud and failure in virtually every area of public life. People have been let down and led astray – to disastrous consequences – by government and politicians, corporations and titans of business, civic leaders and experts of all stripes. Unbelievable lapses of oversight and the alarming lack of foresight have occurred across administrations and on the watch of both parties.

As a consequence, the government *of* the people has rarely been held in such low regard *by* the people; and when the body created by and for the people does not enjoy the public trust, it must be viewed as nothing short of a crisis. We must restore trust in our leaders above all else. Now more than ever, the governmental leaders' role must be accountability for restoring the alliance of rugged individualism and common enterprise so that "we the people" can take back the Dream.

A Sailor in the Ivory Tower

A few years ago I was asked to speak about ethical leadership at Yale University. I told the audience that we have broad challenges, but meeting them begins in the details, the metrics, and our willingness to shape our policies around them. I said that we need leaders who are willing to lose their jobs to say here's where we are, here's what I think we have to do based on the facts, and these are the benchmarks you can judge me by, and if it doesn't work then hold me accountable for my job. In fact, I told them, making a commitment to that type of accountable leadership is, more than any specific policy, what it's going to take to overcome the litany of failures the American people have had to endure for far too long. Finding the problem and fixing it – that's the essence of leadership.

The speech went alright, but the real value came in the question and answer session afterward. These bright young minds, like so many of the other students I had met across Pennsylvania, were unburdened by experience and unafraid to suggest bold ideas. It helped settle in my mind that the best way to test my beliefs and research conclusions was in the classrooms of Pennsylvania's colleges and universities. So, I joined the faculty of Carnegie Mellon University, Cheyney University, Dickinson College, Penn State Law, and the Army War College to teach – and learn in – courses on "Ethical Leadership" and "Restoring the American Dream."

While we studied the dual tenets of America's character in the first course, in the second we applied analysis to determine the best course of policy action within their template for advancing the American Dream. All opinions were to be left at the door. We first examined issues analytically from the perspective of what are the facts, what is your analysis of the issue based on those facts, and based on that analysis how do we move forward to provide for a fair individual opportunity and the commonwealth of our country. Then you can give your opinion of those facts. As I told the students, keep in mind what Napoleon said (and don't tell my wife), "If I were to be in love, I would analyze it bit by bit, because you cannot ask 'how' or 'why' enough."

I had students from all different backgrounds – engineering, liberal arts, active military, Peace Corps, city kids, farm boys, foreign born, and hometown. My students were undergraduates, master's students, and juris doctor candidates. This national treasure of our nation – our youth – took a journey with me to learn.

This book is the culmination of what we learned in those classrooms, what I learned in the Navy and in Congress as a public servant, and what I gained during my years driving around Pennsylvania after the 2010 election to over 600 events listening to the people – laborers, businesspersons, teachers, prison wardens, social workers, healthcare employees, investors, and thousands of other occupations. This book is about the broad challenges I see our nation facing, what I think we must do to meet them, and why I believe the alliance of rugged individualism and the common purpose can restore our American Dream.

Finally, this book is your contract to hold *me* accountable for the results – beginning first with being accountable for the trust of the people.

Joe Sestak

Section II

RESTORING OUR ECONOMY –
BE ALL YOU CAN BE

Chapter 2

THINKING BIG FOR SMALL BUSINESSES

When I was a freshman in Congress, my constituents were impressed when I told them that I had already been selected as Vice Chairman of the Small Business Committee. Then, when I'd tell them how I only got the position because so few Congresspersons wanted to be on the committee, they would look at me in disbelief. How could it be that all of these senior politicians who talk about small business as the "backbone" and "lifeblood" of our economy let a first-term former sailor be Vice Chair?

I could tell you it was because of my Ph.D. in political economy from Harvard or that they recognized I ran the Navy's $70 billion a year requirements directorate (the equivalent of one of the biggest corporations in America) dealing with thousands of small businesses, but the dirty secret is that most politicians have no interest in being on the Small Business Committee because small businesses don't have the funds to make large campaign contributions. There's simply no money in it for elected officials. But their loss was my gain, because when it comes to restoring the American Dream, small business is a big deal. In fact, almost 1 in 5 Americans rank starting their own business as an integral part of the Dream,[2] and about half of Pennsylvania's private sector workforce is employed by or owns a small business.[3]

When it comes to creating jobs for the benefit of our common enterprise, there is no better catalyst than the rugged innovation of America's entrepreneurs and the businesses they build. America's 28 million small businesses might not be represented on the Dow Jones, but they create roughly 70 percent of new jobs. New firm startups alone account for almost 20 percent of gross job creation.[4] And in terms of overall employment, more than half of American jobholders work for firms with 1-500 employees.[5] Small businesses are the engine of our common economic enterprise because they make it possible for the majority of Americans to raise our children well, purchase a home, pay for college, save for retirement, and live a healthy life in a secure nation. But despite the strength and importance of small businesses in our economy, there is evidence that today our entrepreneurs are not able to be all they can be.

As the admiral "CEO" overseeing the Navy's five-year $350-billion-dollar warfare requirements programs, I actually saw what small businesses could do as a force multiplier due to their ingenuity in innovating products and processes. Today, this force multiplier is half of what it was when I was in the Navy. According to Census Bureau data,[6] there were 35 new employer businesses for every 10,000 citizens age sixteen and over in the year 1977. By 1989 that number had dropped to 27. By the 1990s there were fewer than 25 and by the 2000s there were only about 22. By the end of the great recession in 2009, less than 18 new employer businesses were created per 10,000 citizens age sixteen and over – a full 50% drop from 1977 to 2009. An analysis by the *Wall Street Journal* found a similar slump, noting that in 1982 new companies made up roughly half of all American businesses, but today it's only one third.[7] And yet, even with these falling numbers, today's small businesses still create 70 percent of new jobs.

I believe our small businesses and startups are being held back from achieving their full potential. There are a number of factors at work here: access to funding, burdensome regulation, and a government that favors large corporations over small businesses. By looking at these issues through the lens of empowering the rugged entrepreneur to better our common enterprise, there are practical policy solutions to bring our economy back to firing on all cylinders.

Freeing Up Funding

The biggest barrier to an innovator with an idea is a lack of access to capital. It is funding – not tax cuts – that is the mother's milk for a startup. Most small businesses, 7 out of 10, rely on personal savings or assets to begin and expand their business.[8] And because it took twice the share of per capita income for an American to start a business in 2011 as it took in 2006, entrepreneurs today require much greater access to investment capital.[9] If we're serious about job creation and kick-starting the economy, we must make sure that small businesses have greater access to seed money. While the government certainly has a part to play, government also has an opportunity to incentivize private actors to bet on small businesses.

When small businessmen and businesswomen face a funding gap, they can try to attract angel investor financing, venture capital financing, or attempt to secure a bank loan. Angel investors are wealthy individuals who invest in new businesses, usually with the dual intention of creating new companies in their communities and, in so doing, turning a profit for themselves. It is estimated that angel investors with a net worth of at least $1 million directly invested into over 70,000 early-stage companies in 2013.[10]

Venture capital groups, on the other hand, are less likely to get involved in new businesses. Of the roughly 600,000 new business that are started each year, only 1,000 of these businesses receive their first round of funding from venture capital – that's one sixth of one percent of new businesses.[11] However, among startup companies that have made it all the way to the initial public offering stage, over 60 percent have venture capital backing.[12] Angel investors give small businesses their wings, venture capitalists help them fly.

To encourage greater investment in small business by angel investors and venture capital groups, government shouldn't make demands but should instead use tax incentives to make investing in a small company more attractive. We can start by giving angel investors a tax credit for 50 percent of investments made in small businesses during their first five years of operation with an annual limit of $1,000,000. Many states already have similar, more modest tax credits for angel investors and their results speak for themselves.

In 2005, Wisconsin created a tax credit for residents who invested in startups. In 2012 the number of angel-investor groups in Wisconsin had grown from four to more than 20 – and that's *after* going through the great recession.[13] For privately managed venture capital funds, we should provide a similar tax credit that encourages these groups to invest in earlier stages of business development instead of later in the more developed stage of a small business.

By making a shared taxpayer investment in the engine of our economy – rugged innovators – we will share a common dividend in more entrepreneurship, more jobs, and more opportunity.

Small businesses historically have a harder time getting loans from banks than from investors, and this was especially true during the recession when banks weren't willing to lend. From June of 2007 to June of 2011, bank balances of small businesses loans fell 10 percent.[14] This is largely due to the biggest banks lending less money, because over the same period community banks increased their small business loan volume.[15] According to a 2010 Federal Reserve survey, only 6 percent of small business were started using a personal loan from a bank or savings institutions and 3 percent were started using a business loan – significantly lower than before the recession.[16]

This isn't all that surprising – banks *lend*, they don't *invest*. And when lending, a bank needs to see assets to secure the loan. No responsible lender can count an idea alone as an asset. To encourage banks to make loans to small businesses, the Small Business Administration (SBA) has loan guarantee programs that reduce some of the risk for banks that loan to small businesses who would not otherwise qualify for credit. Essentially, taxpayers are willing to bet on small businesses because we know that by empowering innovators to follow their dreams, we all benefit from new jobs, new products, and new competition.

But it isn't a free ride for the banks or the businessmen. To protect this shared investment of ours, the lender has to follow the SBA's standard operating procedures and the SBA charges an upfront guarantee fee plus an annual servicing fee. Some of these fees are often passed on to the borrower. As a benefit to the bank, the guaranteed loans do not count toward the bank's legal lending limit, allowing them to further expand their customer base. It's a good deal for everyone – the taxpayers have a more vibrant economy, banks can make more loans, and entrepreneurs have the opportunity to be all they can be.

Under the SBA's guaranteed loan program there are various special incentives for specific business needs, and expanding many of these programs would allow more small businesses to access more capital and grow more rapidly to create jobs. Much like Lincoln did with the transcontinental railroad, sometimes government has to invest in ideas that corporate interests will not. There are a few specific loan programs that, in my mind, exemplify this balance of rugged individualism and the common purpose, and each of them deserves expansion.[17]

The Rural Lender Advantage Loan guarantees up to 85 percent of a maximum $350,000 in financing to businesses in the rural communities that make up both Pennsylvania's and America's heartland.[18] The $350,000 cap has not been increased since the program was introduced in 2007. We should raise it to $500,000 to ensure that rural communities are not isolated from our continuing recovery. When we invest in a family farmer, we all get more food on our own table and on the world's – and our economy grows as we become the breadbasket of the world.

The Patriot Express Loan is available to military veterans and their spouses. It has the lowest interest rates and guarantees loans up to 85 percent of a maximum $500,000 in financing.[19] This loan for veterans is currently a pilot program, and it should be made permanent with the cap increased to $1,000,000. The men and women applying for these loans have shown that they are committed to putting everything they've got on the line to achieve our common mission. They are exactly the type of rugged individuals we want in our small businesses sector.

We have to make sure that each individual has a fair shot at following his Dream, but studies show that minority small business owners are disproportionately denied credit by banks.[20] If we're going to succeed as a nation in creating a rising economic tide for everyone, minority small business owners need to be given a fair opportunity. President Richard Nixon recognized this when he started the first minority business enterprise program, which was aimed at growing small business opportunities for African American entrepreneurs.[21]

Data from the Small Business Administration (SBA) shows that 80 percent of SBA loan applications from black and Hispanic business owners are for $150,000 or less.[22] Near the end of 2013, the SBA waived the 2 percent loan guarantee fee on loans less than $150,000,[23] and by the summer of 2014 there was already a 15 percent increase in these small loans.[24] The fee waiver should be made permanent so that minority-owned small businesses have a better shot at accessing the capital they need to create jobs in our shared communities.

Through increased SBA loan guarantees and specifically targeted tax incentives for angel investors and venture capital groups, we can allow more entrepreneurs to strike out into the market and create the jobs and goods that benefit our common enterprise. But although both of these ideas require government action, we can also empower small businesses by getting government out of their way.

Responsibly Reducing Regulation

When I think of how burdensome regulations can get in the way of entrepreneurs, I always think of one particular story from my travels across Pennsylvania. I was speaking with a group of supporters who were for the most part practical environmentalists like myself. A man named Russ who happened to run his own small business began telling me about a regulation under the Resource Conservation and Recovery Act (RCRA) that was hurting his business and his customers. The RCRA is an important piece of legislation – among other things, it bans the disposal of hazardous waste in landfills. To do so, waste generators must fill out a land disposal restriction form to notify disposal facilities that they cannot landfill the waste.

Russ explained to me that large companies disposing large amounts of waste make a single notification for each shipment unit, but because of the nature of waste generated in small labs such as his business, each individual lab pack of small vials with chemicals in it is considered a separate unit of waste. Every time a lab disposes, say, 15 to 20 containers, a form has to be filled out for each one.

Making matters worse for Russ, because the law has been in effect since 1976, disposal facilities have begun designing their own individual forms for waste generators to fill out. These forms tell the generators what they already know – the waste cannot be landfilled. As a result, while the company's representative is filling out these 15 to 20 forms at the treatment facility, the packaging crew is sitting around waiting.

Recently, Russ sent me a memo from the American Chemical Society that contained a study they had performed showing that the estimated financial implications of this process are $10 to $15 million a year, conservatively, and not including the cost of paper or mailing. The EPA, meanwhile, had been estimating that the cost was only a couple tens of thousands of dollars. The EPA was off by a factor of close to 1,000.

The irony, of course, is that Russ is himself an avid environmentalist. In fact, he is a volunteer for the EPA's Schools Chemical Cleanout Campaign that helps schools manage and properly dispose of excess or aging materials that are used in chemistry classes. But as a business owner and a man who cares deeply about the environment, Russ sees both sides of the coin. It is crucial that we protect our health and environment from hazardous waste, but the regulations we put in place have to take the concerns of small businesses into account and not be written in a one-size-fits-all fashion.

Proper regulation is often adequately accommodated in a big business from an economic perspective because of the ability to marginalize costs over a large enterprise. Regulation impacts small businesses more simply because the cost cannot be readily marginalized in an enterprise of a few people. The time required to fill out paperwork and file reports, the number of reports, and the cost of compiling information does not vary with the size of the business. As a result, studies have shown that the regulatory costs faced by small businesses with fewer than 20 employees are close to 40 percent higher than those for large firms with 500 employees or more.[25] And as the end result, bigger businesses have a competitive advantage based solely on the government's regulations. This hurts small businesses, but because the uneven cost of regulatory compliance decreases competition, it creates higher prices for everybody. The question must always be whether the cost to a small business is greater than the cost to the common good – including when the original benefits intended by a regulation are, in cases, less affected by a small business activity, anyway.

Creating a system of tiers in regulation is one commonsense solution that comes to mind in ensuring a fair individual opportunity for small businesses. There are a few examples of this across various administrative agencies. For example, the cost of certain filing fees with the SEC varies based on the size of the offering.[26] Under the Federal Insecticide, Fungicide, and Rodenticide Act, small businesses are eligible for a partial registration fee waiver of 50 to 75 percent.[27] Similarly, the Food and Drug Administration will waive the application fee for the first human drug application that a small business submits for review.[28] The U.S. Patent and Trademark Office has an expedited review program that charges lower fees for smaller companies.

This tiered cost system for regulatory fees based on the size of the business helps entrepreneurs across the country. But these agencies aren't coming up with these fee structures on their own. These exceptions can only exist because Congress mandates that agencies do so, and Congress isn't requiring tiered costs often enough (because of the small interest in small business as you could see from me becoming Vice Chairman of the committee).

There is one small department in particular, tucked away in the bureaucracy, that is doing good work for small businesses with a pretty tiny staff. It came into existence as a result of the Regulatory Flexibility Act and the Small Business Regulatory Enforcement Fairness Act

– both signed by Democratic presidents – which require agencies to consider the impact of their regulations on small businesses. But it is the SBA's Office of Advocacy – created by a Republican president – that is tasked with actually making sure agencies are accountable to the language of the legislation. I love it when Democrats have a great idea, but it takes Republicans to make it actually work – true bipartisanship!

With only about a dozen lawyers, a small group of economists, and ten regional advocates, the Office of Advocacy saved small businesses at least $2.5 billion in quantifiable first-year regulatory costs in 2013.[29] From 1998-2009, the office is estimated to have saved small businesses over $200 billion.[30] They do so by combing through proposed regulations, meeting with small businesses, and working with agencies to make sure they're keeping the job-creators in mind while ensuring the fair application of regulation where needed. That's an investment the taxpayers can get behind, and we should look into bolstering and replicating the program in other areas of government to increase small business savings in the coming years.

But small businesses themselves should also have the opportunity to get directly involved in working with regulators to find ways to cut costs while ensuring compliance. Currently, the regulatory rulemaking process is virtually inaccessible to small businesses. After a regulatory agency has crafted a proposed new rule, it is required to publish the rule in the Federal Register and receive comments from interested persons. Then, trade groups and businesses with time to read the Federal Register every day can start poking holes in an agency's proposal. After receiving input from those who spoke up, rules are rewritten to a degree to take the critical comments into consideration. Small business owners who have less time and resources to make comments are almost completely left out of the process.

But there is a better way to try and combat the inefficiencies of the rulemaking process. In 1990 Congress passed the Negotiated Rulemaking Act. This bill was meant to encourage agencies to use a negotiated rulemaking "committee" comprised of up to 25 persons representing the interests of private sector entities affected by agency regulation. That way, industry input could be gained in advance of the comment period, saving time and money on later revisions, with the added benefit of giving regulators insight as to how their ideas would actually affect business.

But although negotiated rulemaking seemed like an excellent idea at the time and was reauthorized in 1996, most agencies simply do not use negotiated rulemaking even though they are authorized to do so.[31] And even on the extremely rare occasion that they do, small businesses are significantly underrepresented in committee seats that go overwhelmingly to industry leaders and special interests.

Congress should amend the Negotiated Rulemaking Act to create greater direction for negotiated rulemaking and require that more of the seats on the negotiation committee are reserved for small business and their representatives. That way, rugged individual business owners like Russ would be more empowered to point out problems with new regulation and find a way to balance the common purpose goals of the agency with the practical needs of the private entrepreneur.

Exports Abroad Means Jobs at Home

It's no coincidence that the American Dream was most within reach when we were still a country that made stuff. Reducing our trade deficit must be a number one priority for our leaders – not just for the sake of a balance sheet, but because every $1 billion of additional exports produces about 7,000 good American jobs.[32] So, just closing our current trade deficit would create around 300,000 jobs. And what's more, it is estimated that trade supported jobs pay 13 to 18 percent higher than the national average wage.[33] More American exports; more American jobs. And if we are serious about being an exporter of everything again, our job-creators in small business are our best bet.

Most banks, however, are not always willing to bet on a non-experienced exporter. Similarly, most insurers aren't willing to take a risk covering a small manufacturer when his overseas buyer isn't yet experienced enough to be perceived as fully creditworthy. Making matters worse, these same entrepreneurs don't even have a level playing field abroad because they're up against foreign businesses whose governments subsidize exports. In fact, there are roughly sixty other nations with agencies that help their own country's businesses finance exports.[34] Chief among them is China, which has been dramatically increasing export credits as U.S. manufacturing becomes more competitive.

The Export-Import Bank of the United States is relatively unknown to most people, but its goal is important: leveling the international playing field to enable American entrepreneurs to turn an export opportunity into an actual sale. The Ex-Im Bank provides businesses engaged in international trade with accounts receivable insurance, guaranteed lines of credit, and direct loans drawn from the Treasury when private banks perceive excess risk. None of these programs are handouts – the Ex-Im Bank charges fees to businesses involved for each service, the proceeds of which are returned back to the Treasury.

Today the White House and the Chamber of Commerce (two groups too often in opposition) both agree that the Ex-Im Bank is good for the budget. According to the White House, the Bank helps American companies "create and support jobs here at home at no cost to taxpayers."[35] Similarly, the Chamber says that the Bank "doesn't cost the American taxpayer a dime."[36] On the other hand, opponents of the Bank who believe the government has no business getting involved in the business-sector point to Congressional Budget Office estimates that show the bank costs taxpayers $200 million a year if proper accounting methods are used.[37]

What neither side takes into account in these numbers are the jobs created by increased exports, which leads to more tax dollars put back into the system. In Pennsylvania alone, the Export Import Bank supported over 250 businesses that conducted a total of $6 billion in transaction since 2007, directly supporting 35,000 jobs in the process.[38] In 2013, the Bank reported that over the preceding 12-month period it approved 3,842 authorizations with an export value of $37.4 billion dollars, which is estimated to have sustained 205,000 export-related American jobs.[39]

Even if we assume that those 205,000 jobs were sustained at the $200 million cost cited by opponents of the Bank, that's an investment of less than $1,000 per job sustained – an investment that generates taxpayers a rapid return from the taxes those job-holders are paying back to the government. Our shared taxpayer investment allows rugged exporters to expand into international markets for our common economic benefit, bringing us that much closer to restoring the American Dream.

I believe that small business owners always have been and will continue to be the bedrock of the American Dream. By having a government that is limited enough to stay out of their way but ambitious enough to clear a path for their success, we will all prosper.

Chapter 3

THE REBIRTH OF AMERICAN MANUFACTURING

After decades of reading the same newspaper stories about factories closing their doors and moving production plants to China, I'm enjoying my morning Joe a lot more now that I'm reading headlines like "GE opens new appliance plant in Louisville, first in 50 years," "Ford bringing jobs back to the U.S. at its Fusion plant," "Caterpillar to relocate production factory from Japan to Athens, Georgia," and "Foreign investors drawn to Western Pennsylvania." Due to a variety of economic factors shifting in our favor, American manufacturing is on the cusp of a comeback.

First and foremost, the cost of labor in emerging economies has risen by double-digit rates. In China, labor costs have risen 15 percent annually for a few years now.[40] Second, there has been a jump in the cost of overseas transportation due to finite freight shipping and the rising cost of diesel fuel.[41] Third, energy prices at home have remained low thanks in large part to our domestic energy boom. Fourth, quality control issues with low-cost foreign-made goods are resulting in high-cost losses in product reputation.

Fifth, in today's economy, customers are more likely to have custom needs that require a speedier supply chain than a cargo ship on the Pacific Ocean can muster. Sixth, companies are finding that manufacturing their products in countries with poor protections from intellectual property rights results in knockoffs that steal their designs. And finally, companies have found that their customers care deeply about purchasing products that are stamped with a proud label – "Made in the USA." When Buck Knives brought production back from Asia to the U.S., their chairman said his customers "don't like anything with that C word on it."[42]

What is most remarkable is that the recent re-shoring wave only accounted for 50,000 of the 520,000 new manufacturing jobs added from 2010 to 2013.[43] This isn't just a matter of big corporations coming home; and while many of these jobs were the direct result of the recession ending, they also include a growing rebirth of American manufacturing in small- and medium-sized firms. According to data from the Bureau of Labor Statistics and the Census, 98 percent of America's manufacturing firms are small[44] and the average manufacturing business has fewer than 50 employees.[45] So while it's welcome news that mature, multi-national manufacturers like Ford, Caterpillar, and GE are coming back home, it's the rugged innovators in small businesses that will be the future face of American manufacturing, creating quality jobs and putting the Dream back in reach for millions.

There is much that we the people can do through government to allow the initiative and enterprise of the new manufacturing sector to prosper, creating more jobs and opportunities for our shared common purpose. One item I have already talked about is smarter regulation for small businesses, which includes manufacturers. Other areas of importance are investing in infrastructure so that manufacturers can move people and products faster, retraining our workforce to close the skills gap in the new Made in America sector, and creating a tax environment that incentivizes research and development – or R&D – investment. Each of these last three topics will be addressed at length in later chapters. Here, in this chapter, I want to talk about actions we should take to capitalize on advantages unique to America, allowing our manufacturers to be all they can be to benefit from our shared economic enterprise.

Growing Jobs through Green Energy

Job growth comes from innovation, and innovating is what America does best. Unfortunately, over the last decade, our international competitors have become very adept at putting our American inventions to better use than we have. For example, the first electricity-generating wind turbine was invented in Cleveland, Ohio, to provide energy to remote farmers and ranchers.[46] Yet, as I saw while in Congress, the leading wind energy companies in my state, Gamesa and Iberdola, are both Spanish-owned.

Similarly, solar energy was invented in America,[47] yet China now boasts the world's largest solar panel industry that exports 95 percent of its production, including to the United States.[48] In fact, the Chinese government offers its solar panel manufacturers low-cost credit, free land and utilities, and discount materials.[49] They can afford to do so because they are literally stealing our technology from us – China's People's Liberation Army recently had a hacker steal thousands of files from SolarWorld's Oregon manufacturing plant.[50]

It's just plain wrong that our elected leaders have allowed Europe and China to use our own technology to get in front of us globally. But restoring American's position as the global leader in the green energy sector isn't about nationalist chest-pounding or merely environmentalist tree-hugging – it's about creating jobs. According to one analysis, for every $1 million of output expenditures, one job is created in the oil and natural gas industries. In the coal industry, two jobs are created. By contrast, for every $1 million investment in the wind industry, 4.5 jobs are produced, and the numbers rise to 5.4 jobs for solar and 7.4 for biomass.[51]

The reason that green energy creates more jobs is because more of the $1 million is spent in the manufacturing sector, which requires more labor than extracting and transporting fossil fuels. In fact, according to the Brookings Institute, more than 1 in 4 green energy jobs are in manufacturing compared to less than 1 in 10 in the broader economy.[52] And these are good, family-sustaining jobs that have been the backbone of this country for decades, like machinist, sheet metal worker, welder, and electrician. In 1922, my grandfather emigrated with his son – my father – from Czechoslovakia and, seizing on the rising promise of the American Dream, became a steelworker in Coatesville, Pennsylvania. Today, many of the workers in Pennsylvania's wind industry are members of the United Steelworkers.

Aside from direct and indirect job creation, there are various secondary benefits to lighting up our green energy sector. One is that as the renewable energy sector grows and costs continue to go down, our cost-of-energy advantage over our international competitors will continue to increase. That means more business owners will decide to keep their production plants here at home instead of sending them overseas. Then there's the fact that more green jobs means less carbon emitted. That isn't just good for the environment; it's good for our economy. Lowering factories' fossil fuel emissions means fewer premature deaths and fewer cases of respiratory illness, which means fewer days of work will be missed and the workforce will be more productive – while also lessening the burden on our health care system. And gains in productivity means an even greater American economic advantage.

What can we do to accelerate the growth of green energy stamped "Made in America" and the jobs that come with it? Some may not like it when I say this, but when I think about how government can aid rugged individuals in an emerging industry for the benefit of our common enterprise, I look to the origins of hydraulic fracturing as an example.

In 1975, energy executives told President Gerald Ford that they feared conventional natural gas resources were going to run out. To get ahead of the problem, government partnered with the private sector to find solutions. The Department of Energy sponsored industry research to estimate the volume of natural gas in unconventional reservoirs like shale.[53] The Energy Research and Development Administration developed diamond-tipped drill bits for geothermal energy that were then used by the natural gas industry.[54] Even the U.S. Navy aided the natural gas industry when the undersea sonar technology we created to track Russian submarines was repurposed to allow drillers to track shale deposits underground.[55]

To incentivize companies to explore unconventional gas extraction methods, Congress passed the Natural Gas

Policy Act in 1978, deregulating wellhead sales prices and adjusting price ceilings.[56] Later, in 1980, Congress passed the Crude Oil Windfall Profits Tax Act, which provided tax credits for gas produced through 2002.[57] As a result of government aiding the rugged individuals in the industry, natural gas has become a cheap, reliable source of domestic energy from which we all prosper – to the tune of 25 trillion cubic feet per year.[58]

But just as we don't want people to be on welfare forever, we don't want an industry on corporate welfare forever. The billions of dollars in tax credits, deductions, and exceptions that exist for the benefit the oil and gas industry should be quickly phased out.[59] Many of these exceptions go far beyond encouragement of an industry to endangering public health – with the "Halliburton loophole" exemption of natural gas extraction fluids from regulation under the Clean Water Act. It is because of policies like the Halliburton loophole that I greatly fear that Pennsylvanians will be "left behind" once the natural gas companies are done drilling, and may have an even greater cost to bear than we did from coal mining. Drilling can ensure a common good by offering reduced carbon emissions and less dependence on foreign oil, but it must not be at a greater cost, or even damage, to our Commonwealth.

Oil and gas companies have been nurtured by government for half a century, and now that they are mature industries they shouldn't get a free lunch that we're paying for through tax expenditures, lasting losses in land values, and also medical bills from air pollution and, at times, poisoned water. We must end the subsidies for the hydraulic fracturing industry, and then we should follow the successful pattern set out by the history of that industry and use the tools of government to aid rugged innovation in the new green energy sector for the benefit of our common enterprise – always with the future goal of again cutting the cord once the green energy industry has matured.

We can start by restoring for a predictable term the renewable electricity Production Tax Credit (PTC) and the Investment Tax Credit (ITC) which Congress let expire and later renewed retroactively for only 2014. The PTC provides a 2.3 cent-per-kilowatt-hour tax credit for wind, geothermal, and closed-loop biomass and a 1.1 cent/kWh credit for other eligible technologies. The ITC is worth up to 30 percent of developing solar energy, fuel cells, and wind turbines, and 10 percent of expenditures on geothermal systems.[60] Congress keeps letting these tax credits expire over and over again, only to later grant one or two year extensions after creating uncertainty across the green energy industry. Congress should renew the PTC and ITC through 2020 to give the industry the long-term certainty it needs to grow.

Similarly, the Research and Development Tax Credit that expired at the end of 2013 was at the last minute renewed for 2014. It has expired and been extended 15 times since 1981, creating great uncertainty for businesses,[61] especially in our manufacturing sector, which is responsible for 70 percent of R&D.[62] We should make the R&D Tax Credit permanent, but we need to do more to make small businesses aware of its existence. According to the *Wall Street Journal*, the vast majority of eligible small businesses do not take advantage of the R&D tax credit.[63] Our leaders need to stop bragging about their votes to support greater R&D and start actually working with small businesses in their districts to make sure they claim the benefits that their big business peers are monopolizing.

Our history has shown that government can aid rugged individuals in an emerging industry for the benefit of our common enterprise. If it worked for hydraulic fracturing, it can work for windmills and solar panels. And in doing so, it can help put American manufacturing back to work, too. The green energy manufacturing sector is just one of many examples of how concerns over the environment, climate change, and energy security can touch almost every policy issue we face in this country, which is why I will address some of these concerns throughout this book as opposed to isolating them in a single chapter. In fact, because I see these issues as matters of national security, I address climate change and energy security in my national security chapter later in the book. These issues are not only vital to U.S. security interests, but climate change is the number one strategic livable issue for our world.

Strengthening Intellectual Property Rights

The alliance of rugged individualism and the common enterprise was beautifully expressed by our founders in the Patent and Copyright Clause of the Constitution, which grants Congress the power "To promote the Progress of Science and useful Arts, by securing for limited Times to Authors and Inventors the exclusive Right to their respective Writings and Discoveries." By using government as a force for good to empower and protect innovators, we all benefit from the shared advances in technology and knowledge. Our founders knew then, just as our business owners know now, that innovation isn't possible unless ideas are protected.

Strong intellectual property rights are critically important to manufacturers and small business owners. In fact, nine out of ten patents in the U.S. come from the manufacturing sector,[64] and small businesses produce 13 times more patents per employee than large businesses.[65]

However, inventors with ideas are finding themselves in a holding pattern with the U.S. Patent and Trademark Office (USPTO). As of February 2014, the USPTO's 8,000 patent examiners faced a backlog of over 600,000 patent applications, with an average total time before final disposition of the application taking 28 months.[66] That's down significantly from 2009, when the backlog was sitting at 1.2 million applications and final disposition took 3.5 years.[67] But even with the improvements, capital investors are less likely to advance their money if they know a patent application will be sitting in place for years.

The America Invents Act has made decent progress in making our patent system work better for innovators. Since its passage, various pilot programs have been developed, including a program that uses veteran patent examiners as coaches for their junior colleagues and another that brings in outside experts from the private sector to provide examiners with cutting-edge technical knowledge.[68] The USPTO has also adding satellite offices across the country, with two already in place in Detroit and Denver and another two planned for Dallas and in Silicon Valley. And because the USPTO now gets to keep the funding from patent fees, these offices exist at little or no cost to the taxpayer.[69]

More can still be done to speed up the process and reduce the backlog, and the most immediate way to do so is by hiring more examiners. This can be done at little or no expense to the taxpayer by making a slight tweak to one of USPTO's already-successful programs. Currently, applicants who want a speedy disposition of their application can file for "Prioritized Examination," which incurs a fee of $4,000 for non-small entities, $2,000 for small entities, and $1,000 for micro-entities. It's a good example of tiered pricing by a regulatory agency. The total number of these prioritized applications is capped at 10,000 per year. On average, final disposition of applications with prioritized status took just 6.5 months.[70]

As the Prioritized Examination program shows, the patent approval system can work quickly when the right resources are applied. So, to expand this success to the overall patent system, the fee for big businesses ("non-small entities") should be doubled for prioritized applications, and the added revenue should go toward hiring additional examiners. And as more examiners are hired, the 10,000 per year cap on prioritized applications can be raised, which will in turn lead to more revenue for the USPTO and a reduced backlog on innovation, from which we all benefit.

While we must do everything we can to make our own system work well for our entrepreneurs with ideas, we also have to do everything in our power to hold our international competitors accountable for the theft of our intellectual property. The former National Security Agency Director, General Keith Alexander, was correct when he called this international thievery "the greatest transfer of wealth in history." According to a statistical analysis performed by the International

Trade Commission, if intellectual property protection in China improved substantially, over 2 million jobs would be added to the U.S. economy.[71] To get China to take intellectual property seriously, we have to show how serious we are about protecting our innovators.

Fortunately, a number of forward-thinking American leaders of all stripes have already started to search for solutions. For example, the Commission on the Theft of American Intellectual Property recently developed a series of recommendations to hold international thieves and counterfeiters accountable. I support many of these recommendations, which include sequestering imported goods that incorporate stolen intellectual property and requiring companies to comply with intellectual property laws in order to gain access to the U.S. financial system or be listed on U.S. stock exchanges. Without question, the only way to force our competition to play fair is to make it too costly for them to break the rules. This is something that we must do – for the sake of our jobs and future prosperity here at home.

Chapter 4

Investing in Our Infrastructure

A merica's achievements in infrastructure are some of
our proudest historical triumphs – the Erie Canal,
the Transcontinental Railroad, the Golden Gate Bridge,
and the Interstate Highway System. These public work
projects – admired, studied, and envied around the world
– have always stood as physical monuments to that great
American idea that, together, we can defy gravity, rise
higher, and each one of us go further. But today, our
infrastructure is crumbling all around us – much of it in
urgent need of repair, improvement, and reinvestment.

Today, on America's major highways, congestion costs
the economy over $100 billion annually in wasted work
hours and fuel, and the poor condition of our roads costs
individual drivers $324 per year in car repairs.[72] Over
66,000 of America's bridges are structurally deficient,
requiring significant maintenance or replacement.[73]
Pennsylvania, my home state, ranked 41st in overall
highway performance in 2012, and it was one of the seven
states with one-third of their bridges officially reported
as deficient.[74]

Our roads are, of course, only one part of the story.

Our nation's freight rail infrastructure, in order to
accommodate future economic growth, must be able to
handle the estimated 88 percent increase in tonnage by

2035.[75] In our skies, congestion and delays cost us over $22 billion per year.[76] Our seaports are in need of updating and expansion to take in the larger ships sailing across the Atlantic and Pacific that carry goods for American exporters and consumers alike. Our inland waterways remain constantly troubled by unscheduled delays and service interruptions at 90 percent of locks and dams, costing hundreds of millions of dollars annually.[77] A newer form of infrastructure – cyber – similarly faces challenges: millions of rural Americans are without access to broadband internet, and those with access in urban areas are paying higher bills for lower speeds than our international competitors.[78]

If we want to maintain our dominant global economic position, then it is crucial that we make the necessary investments in our infrastructure so that we can move people and products into, out of, and around the country. But we have to move fast because we're already falling behind other nations. According to the 2013 World Economic Forum's Global Competitiveness Report, the U.S. ranks 25th in overall quality of infrastructure behind countries such as South Korea, Japan, Canada, Germany, France, and Singapore.[79] But if we make the effort to reinvest in our infrastructure – whether highways, seaports, airports, rails, or broadband internet – I am confident that we will out-compete any nation while creating many quality jobs here at home.

To be sure, the needed investment will not come cheap, but the returns will be significant for our nation's economic strength; The American Society of Civil Engineers recommends an additional investment of $157 billion a year through 2020, which would protect more than $3 trillion in GDP, $2.4 trillion in consumer spending, over $1 trillion in trade, $3,100 in household income, and 3.5 million jobs.[80] Indeed, a Department of Transportation study found that for every $1 billion invested in infrastructure, between 27,000 and 37,000 jobs are created.[81] Based on research done by the Bureau of Labor Statistics, about 80 percent of those jobs will be in the construction, manufacturing, and retail/wholesale trade sectors – and nearly 9 out of 10 of them will be middle class jobs that pay good wages.[82] These are good American jobs, impossible to outsource because everything is built at home.

In short, this is about more than connecting communities for commerce; this is about rebuilding the middle class and putting the American Dream back within reach. But because so much is at stake, we have to make sure that we do it the right way. And right now, we're not.

Government Needs a Better Way to Fund Infrastructure

The way we fund the Interstate Highway System has remained unchanged since 1956. Currently, we use an 18.4 cents per gallon tax on gasoline and a 24.4 cents per gallon tax on diesel to fund our Highway Trust Fund, which, along with funds from individual states, pays for the maintenance, repair, and construction of roads. The 18.4 and 24.4 cent per gallon tax has remained the same since 1993 – when a gallon of gas cost $1.16.[83] And because the fee has remained unchanged for more than 20 years, the purchasing power of the tax has declined dramatically. Due to inflation alone, 18.4 cents buys 30 percent less today than it did in 1993. At the same time, the cost of construction has not gone down.

Another reason why the per-gallon user-fee has become untenable is the failure to anticipate the consequences of an otherwise good policy: fuel efficient vehicles. Fuel economy standards requiring car manufacturers to produce vehicles with greater miles per gallon is good for both our environment and our pocketbook. But because we set up our highway fund as a user fee based on gallons of gas purchased, we now have an unequal system where, because I drive a hybrid car, I'm paying less into the Highway Trust Fund than people who drive the exact same amount of miles that I do but in a less-fuel-efficient vehicle. People who drive electric cars get an even better deal.

As a result of our failure to act with foresight and make our laws adaptable to the changing economic conditions and even welcomed technological advances, Congress has had to bail out the Interstate Highway Fund over and over again in last-minute piecemeal provisions, transferring well over $50 billion from the general fund to the Trust Fund since 2008.[84] And this (literal) free-rider problem will only get worse as the average fuel economy standard goes from 36.5 mpg in 2017 to 54.5 in 2025.[85] A variety of policy options have been proposed to address this problem. Unfortunately, some of the proposed solutions have been typical, unimaginative, Washington DC-style public relations gimmicks, while others are only short-term solutions.

For example, Senators Harry Reid and Rand Paul want to give multinational corporations a tax holiday to repatriate their money stored in offshore accounts at a substantially discounted tax rate, and then funnel the tax revenue into the Highway Fund.[86] House Speaker John Boehner, on the other hand, wants to shore up the fund by cutting mail delivery and sending the savings over.[87] Some in Congress have proposed boosting the fund by temporarily letting corporations underfund their employee's pension plans, generating a one-time source of tax funding. These are all temporary solutions that don't make much long-term sense.

Worse yet, there are some who want to make individual states responsible for their own transportation networks and take the federal government out of the interstate highway business entirely. They want to do this even though it defeats the purpose of having a coordinated interstate system. Every state in the continental United States would find itself mired in the inefficiencies caused by its neighbors. And truck traffic states like North Dakota or Montana would be unable to fund their infrastructure, potentially putting a serious gap in our coast-to-coast transportation system.[88]

The truth is that, because of the nature of our infrastructure funding problem, we need both short-term measures and long-term solutions. All of them, whether short-term or long-term, must be based in the reality that infrastructure is a common good from which we all benefit. From a public policy standpoint, it is practically irrelevant whether we are daily drivers or merely the occasional weekend road trip renters; reliable infrastructure gets the goods to market that we purchase and all of us benefit from the garbage truck using our roads to pick up trash. The same can be said, indeed, of the importance of maintaining world class systems for our traffic at sea, in the air, and over the cyberspace.

At the same time, those who just want to tax our way out of the problem must realize that increased prices at the pump mean higher delivery costs for consumers of all kinds, an impact on small businesses from material costs for their own internal fuel bills, and an overall increase in financial strain on middle class family budgets. We must never forget that taxing gasoline is as much a user fee as it is a regressive tax.

The Road to Resolution

An effective way to work toward fixing our highway funding challenges must be thoughtful and comprehensive, one that recognizes the necessity of short-term measures as we strive to find long-term solutions by balancing competing policy interests. An infrastructure bank can be part of the solution; and whenever possible we must invite private sector entities to play their respective roles as key stakeholders in our efforts to reinvest and rebuild our infrastructure.

In the short-term, we are going to have to address the gasoline tax to make the Highway Trust Fund solvent, with the ultimate goal of eliminating or greatly lowering the tax in the future as long-term solutions become feasible. A recent bipartisan proposal would have raised the gas tax by six cents per year for two years, and then indexed the rate to inflation. Although this bill was supported by a diverse range of prominent groups, including the U.S. Chamber of Commerce, AAA, and the American Trucking Association, it garnered no traction in Congress because practically every legislator expected it to die in the House, where the "No Tax Pledge" had, to the detriment of our nation's long-term growth, become the 11th Commandment. As a result, Congress had no other choice but to transfer money from the general fund – a tax by other means – to keep infrastructure projects from halting. This is an imperfect solution brought about because of a failure of both parties to work together for the benefit of our rugged individuals who use the roads and our common economic enterprise that benefits from increased commerce. For the sake of our ability to regain our competitive footing in a highly networked and dynamic global economy, we must adopt a bipartisan plan such as described above for the short term.

In the meantime, individual states – which also charge a gas tax separate from the federal government's – should begin to experiment with a mileage-based user fee instead of a gallon-based user fee. The gallon-based user fee was intended to be egalitarian when it began in the 1950s, and it made sense because cars generally got the same poor gas mileage. Today, with electric, hybrid, and conventional cars all on the road, the gallon-based fee makes little sense, and a mileage-based fee would go a long way toward making the tax less regressive.

This mileage fee could be tracked in many states by adding an odometer reading to vehicle inspections, and assessing a fee based on actual distance traveled. Eventually, once states have developed successful models, the federal government could eliminate the gasoline tax altogether and restore the Highway Trust Fund to a truly usage-based revenue stream.

Finally, we need to create a national infrastructure bank to finance surface, water, and airway projects. Such a bank would use public money and loan guarantees to attract private capital to support market-based investments – in partnership with local, state, and multi-state entities. These loans would each be guaranteed by revenue from end-users (drivers, airlines, etc) of the finished projects. For this special mix of public-private effort to work, this bank should be a publicly-supported agency with government oversight and a president and governing members appointed by the Senate. And the projects chosen for investment by the bank should be determined based on merit, not on the power of individual senior Senators sitting on special committees.

This infrastructure bank is based not on the idea that government needs to be more involved in infrastructure spending – it does – but on the idea that public resources are scarce and we must generate the proper incentives in order to bring in private sector partners as investors in our shared national venture.

Public-Private Partnerships (PPPs)
Can Work Better Than Government Alone

I believe we should have a government that can do things increasingly in conjunction with private industry, so long as there are benchmarks for accountability along the way. Infrastructure is a particularly good example of how the private and public sectors can work together to achieve mutual benefits. The issue is simple enough: we want certain things but we don't have sufficient funds. Private investors have funds but they also want to make a profit. So, in exchange for the investor providing for the construction, operation, or maintenance of a roadway, airway, or levee, a profit is generated in the form of a toll or fee to the end-user.

All parties win: local, state, and federal bodies get the infrastructure their constituents need at a low cost; private investors make a profit from their venture; and consumers can transport themselves and their goods for a reasonable fee based on use instead of broad taxation.

Although PPPs are relatively new in the infrastructure market, there have already been many success stories from allowing investors to join with government and create an improved system from which we all commonly benefit. In 2006, Indiana leased its system of toll roads to a concession company for 75 years in exchange for $3.8 billion dollars. The Indiana Toll Road Concession Company must maintain the roads, and the company gets the revenue from the tolls. With the $3.8 billion influx, Indiana was able to fund the improvements and repairs in its ten year "Major Moves" initiative, making Indiana the only state to have a fully-funded transportation plan through 2015.

The Chicago Skyway Bridge is another example of a PPP that is working for the benefit of both the investor and the public. For $1.83 billion (the equivalent of 70 percent of the city's budget), the Skyway Concession Company leased the Chicago Skyway for 99 years, allowing Chicago to pay off other infrastructure debts and make improvements elsewhere at the same time. A study performed by the Congressional Budget Office found that for both the Indiana Toll Road and the Chicago Skyway, costs were reduced by about 10 percent under private management.[89] The projects also led to increased bond ratings for Chicago and Indiana, and Standard and Poor's upgraded Indiana's debt rating to AAA, its best rating in history.

Additionally, more focused forms of PPPs have been used to address specific problems such as traffic congestion. For example, the Virginia Department of Transportation joined with private entities under an 85-year, $1.9 billion contract to create four High-Occupancy Toll (HOT) lanes along the I-495 Capital Beltway. The toll prices in the express lanes change according to traffic conditions so that demand is regulated and the lanes are kept relatively free of congestion at all times. To encourage even less congestion, buses and carpools with three or more people ride in the new lanes for free.

With an annual additional need for $157 billion dollars in transportation investment, it is crucial that we leverage infrastructure innovators in the private sector. Government simply cannot go it alone. A shared investment and partnership is the most appropriate path forward because when it comes to our roads, bridges, waterways, seaports, airways, and rail lines, we are all in this together.

Job Growth Depends on Our Wired Infrastructure Too

In the 21st century global economy, each American's ability to access high speed internet is just as important as his or her access to good roads. High speed internet is crucial for entrepreneurs in every corner of the country – they need it to market their products to consumers coast-to-coast and across the oceans. Even as library budgets are being slashed by state legislatures and city halls, the internet provides a unique source of unlimited inquiry for students thirsty for knowledge. And with more than 80 percent of Fortune 500 companies requiring online job applications in 2012, both our workforce and our employers are relying on greater access to the internet.[90] In fact, research has shown that for every 1 percentage point increase in broadband penetration, employment increases by 0.2 to 0.3 percent per year.[91]

And yet, though we invented the internet, our international competitors are able to provide their people with faster speeds at lower costs. This lost opportunity in homegrown technology is not unlike what we saw with the wind turbine and the solar panel industries. In 2013, a 150Mbps (megabits per second) connection from Verizon's FiOS in U.S. cities cost $130 per month, compared to a cost of $50 per month internationally, with consumers in Hong Kong getting 500Mbps for just $25. And while less than 10 percent of households in the United States have access to high-speed optical fiber lines, more than half of South Korean households use this technology. How did we let ourselves get so far behind?

Currently, access to low-cost, high-speed internet is being hindered by a nationwide duopoly in the telecommunications market. With over 22 million subscribers, NBC Comcast controls the wired market in 16 of the top 25 U.S. cities, earning them the title in 2012 as "the communications equivalent of Standard Oil." Their main "competitor," Time Warner, has more than 12 million subscribers and controls most of the remaining regions.[92] And even though the two make up a national telecom duopoly, each has a near monopoly in the areas where they operate. In fact, 50 percent of end users have only two choices for a broadband internet provider where they live, and an additional 20 percent live in an area with only one provider.[93] That means that 70 percent of the population lives in an area with little or no competition between cable companies.

But it's about to get even worse – Comcast announced at the beginning of 2014 that they would buy Time Warner, giving even greater monopoly control over internet service.[94] Instead of private sector competition working for the common enterprise, consumers are likely to continue experiencing poor service, little innovation, high prices, and unacceptably low speeds.

And just as Standard Oil had a strangle hold on our nation's politicians at the beginning of the last century, this century's "public servants" are equally beholden to the titans of telecoms. About 20 states have passed laws backed by cable companies that bar cities from building their own broadband networks to compete with the regional monopoly.[95] Chattanooga, the Tennessee city that created its own fiber optic network, offers speeds at 100 times the national average for about $70 a month. Unsurprisingly, Comcast fought the city's efforts at every turn.[96]

At the federal level, when some states began passing their own cybersecurity laws requiring service providers to protect customers' electronic information, a bill was introduced in the Senate to create a shockingly low national standard requiring companies only to take "reasonable measures" to safeguard data and report breaches directly to customers only when the cost of notification isn't "excessive."[97] Similarly, when the Bring Jobs Home Act was introduced in the Senate to close a tax loophole for companies claiming tax deductions for sending jobs overseas, it was filibustered to death in part so that telecom companies could continue to outsource their call centers to Southwest Asia. Most shockingly, too many members of Congress have vehemently opposed net neutrality – the concept that internet service providers treat all content, sites, and platforms equally.

The bottom line is that Washington's public servants are rewarding internet providers' inadequate performance with tax breaks, sweetheart deals, and lax regulation that does not benefit the consumer. Rather than acquiescing to the cable companies, we should be holding them accountable for letting us slip from being the first nation to develop the internet to having one of the worst speeds of all developed nations – and at one of the highest costs. Instead of encouraging call center outsourcing in our tax code, we should create incentives and rewards for companies that provide higher speeds at lower costs or that enlarge the digital capacity of crucial community institutions like schools and hospitals. And instead of standing by while inefficient and job-killing monopolies grow, we should be expanding our broadband infrastructure to create good-paying jobs and wired-in communities.

Of all communities, those in rural areas of our country are especially in need of greater internet access. In fact, while nearly 100 percent of urbanites have internet access in some form or another, over one-fifth of people in rural areas can barely access the web. That's a big deal for places like my home state, Pennsylvania, which has the third-highest rural population in the country at just over 2.7 million.[98] But expansion of rural broadband isn't just about lending a hand to those left behind in the digital revolution, it's about maintaining America's agricultural sector and preserving farming as a way of life, and retaining and attracting other types of business.

In 2014, Congress took a step in the right direction by finally creating a pilot program for gigabit internet projects in rural areas. This program could be immensely beneficial to rural populations, providing information to the farmers who produce the food resources on which our country thrives, for example. Farmers could easily access weather and climate projections, new techniques for caring for their plants and animals, and tools for banking, health care, and other necessary small business applications. This will go a long way for farmers – who are small business owners – but it will also pay dividends to our shared prosperity. According to the Department of Agriculture (USDA), agriculture is tied to one in 12 American jobs and provides us with 80 percent of the food we consume. The National Agricultural Statistics Service reports that there are 2.1 million farms in America, with 62,100 in Pennsylvania alone. In 2012, agriculture brought in a net income of $114 billion – up from $85 billion in 2008.[99]

The program will also go a long way toward helping rural communities that are experiencing outmigration, strengthening their ability to retain jobs and talent by better integrating these communities into the modern market place. A 2011 U.S. computer and internet use study showed that more than four out of five Americans between the ages of 18 and 44 use the Internet at home. The fact that this is the exact demographic group that is leaving our farming communities should be a surprise to no one – like everyone else, they are looking for growth and opportunities. For the long-term health and sustainability of our rural communities, and thus our nation's economic future, policymakers have a duty to help ensure that these areas remain commercially attractive, economically competitive, and fully integrated with the wider world. We want to retain a fresh young crop of agricultural and other types of entrepreneurs and rural dwellers who are networked and wired, ready to feed our nation with the greatest degree of efficiency possible.

We must expand our broadband infrastructure so we can help these communities spur greater job creation and talent retention. This pilot program is a good, promising start, but we must continuously strive to do more, because strong and reliable infrastructure capable of connecting our people and nation is a key ingredient for America's success – and rural communities, as important contributors to our country's economic vibrancy, are valuable threads in our national fabric.

Throughout our history, we have always thrived as a nation because committed, farsighted, and conscientious leaders always worked toward fostering an environment within which our people and companies can do well and succeed. We moved goods in ways that the world had never known by charting a daring canal; we networked a continent from sea to sea with an epic railroad; and, we looked out to the world with pride from the monumental Golden Gate, which still, to this day, symbolizes our vibrancy, creativity, and "can-do" attitude that made us great. Our history does not end here. Today, as in yesterday, we need leaders who are able to look to the future, providing us with the infrastructure and systems that we need to thrive in our own time.

Chapter 5

Raising Wages, Not Just the Minimum Wage

꿈

Pundits and politicians from my party spend a lot of time on TV talking about raising the minimum wage. It's an important issue and deserves immediate action. But it also doesn't capture the bigger picture. The *median* wage – the wage earned exactly in the *middle* of the wage distribution – has been stagnant for decades. *Real* wages – a measure of income that takes inflation and purchasing power into consideration – peaked 40 years ago.[100] And although productivity has soared over the same period, workers' paychecks have not shared in that productivity in terms of increasing wages for the vast majority of American working families.

Resolving the substantial structural problems our economy has experienced over the last half century, in truth, is about a lot more than raising the minimum wage. Many leaders have made it look as though by increasing the minimum wage we can solve all of our economic problems. It is absolutely true that a higher floor for wages will reduce economic *inequality*, but what we must be truly focused on is economic *mobility* – in which raising the minimum wage is only a starting point.

If we're serious about restoring our economy through greater mobility, the solution isn't just soaking the rich as some in our national dialogue seem to insist. Instead, it's about many of the items already mentioned: creating more small businesses through smarter regulation and greater access to capital so entrepreneurs can create more competition for labor, benefiting us all; encouraging the rebirth of American manufacturers to increase the amount of good paying blue and green collar jobs in a growing sector; and investing in our infrastructure to connect markets and put the transportation sector back to work. It's also about training an agile, better-educated, healthier, more productive workforce; modernizing our tax code; and reasserting our global security position (more on that later).

The bottom line is this: when we talk about raising wages, we have to see the whole forest instead of fixating on the single minimum wage tree. Let's look at the facts.

Fact one: less than 3 percent of American workers are paid the minimum wage.[101] So when we talk about minimum wage workers, we are talking about less than 4 million of the 134 million American workers.

Fact two: the Walmarts and McDonalds aren't paying minimum wage – they are paying very low wages. The average Walmart associate makes $8.81 cents (although Walmart tries to claim it is $12.78).[102][103]

Fact three: The percentage of workers making at or below (below is legal in some areas of labor) minimum wage has gone down almost every year since 1980.[104] That does not, however, say anything about the purchasing power of a particular year's minimum wage – although it is worth noting that the real value of today's minimum wage is two-thirds what it was in 1968.[105]

Fact four: A lot of employers who pay their workers the minimum wage do so because they are struggling as a startup small business, not because they are callous mega-corporations.[106] So, the Republicans aren't entirely wrong to raise hell about *how* raising the minimum wage would affect small business owners – because it *does* depend on *how much* the minimum wage is raised.

Now, let's look at some more facts, this time about the *median* wage in our nation.

Fact one: the median real wage – the wage earned in the middle of the wage distribution in dollars of constant purchasing power – increased by a total of just 5 percent from 1979 to 2012.[107] That's less than one seventh of one percent each year. In contrast, for the top 1 percent of earners the median real wage increased 154 percent, while for the bottom 10th percentile the median real wage fell 6 percent.[108]

Fact two: from 1947 to 1980, hourly compensation rose at the same rate as productivity.[109] Since then, productivity has grown at double the annual rate of compensation, resulting in a 40 percent gap.[110] Workers are putting in as much sweat as ever without receiving a greater return. It's worth noting, however, that while wage growth has been stagnant at roughly 2 percent per year, manufacturing wage growth today has risen to 2.6 percent, giving further merit to my argument that we must invest in that sector.[111]

Fact three: in 1980, only 39 percent of married families with children had both parents working; today that number has risen to 60 percent.[112][113] As a result, a family today with two breadwinners is working harder and earning less in real income. In fact, since 1999 the median level of household income has declined about $4,000 in real terms.[114]

Fact four: the median level of income refers to the exact middle, meaning that if the very middle is hurting, the *majority* is hurting. To restore the American Dream, our energy should be more focused on growing our economy so that *all* wages can grow again. To do so, there are concrete steps that must be taken. Quickly, and based on facts.

Raising the Minimum Wage as a First Step

When I entered Congress in 2007, the year the recession began, the second vote I took was to raise the minimum wage by $1.40 to $7.25 an hour. I did so recognizing an important fact: this first increase of the minimum wage in 10 years was still less than the minimum wage in 1968 when adjusted for inflation ($10.74). The reduction in the real value of the minimum wage from half a century ago is particularly tough today because the majority of those working for minimum or low wages are no longer young teenagers. For instance, 68 percent of fast-food workers are adults, of whom over a quarter have children. And 65 percent are women, all working longer for less. Clearly, something has to be done.

In our policy conversations about wages, we hear some argue that hiking the wage will cause people to lose their jobs since the cost to business will increase. Others argue that a minimum-wage increase will boost the economy and decrease poverty, thereby reducing reliance on taxpayer-funded assistance such as Medicaid and food stamps. But what we're missing from both groups is pragmatic leadership where accountable leaders actually look at the facts and explain why their policy is based on factual information, not ideology. I support raising the national minimum wage to exactly $10.12. Here is why, based on the facts.

Fact one: conclusive studies show that if a minimum wage does not exceed 50 percent of the average hourly wage, people will not lose their jobs.[115] This is primarily because the cost of the wage increase is less to a business owner than having to keep training new people because lower wages mean higher turnover.[116]

Fact two, the current federal minimum wage of $7.25 an hour is about one third of the average hourly wage in America ($22.53).[117] Therefore, we could raise the minimum wage to $10.12 (50 percent of the average hourly wage) and people would not lose their jobs.

Fact three – and proof of the 50 percent rule – there are a number of case studies that show no job loss when the minimum wage was raised, as long as it was not above 50 percent of the average hourly wage. One study involving data from Pennsylvania[118] examined fast- food restaurants in New Jersey that raised the minimum wage to 47 percent of the average hourly wage, and there was no evidence of any job loss when compared to fast-food restaurants across the border in southeastern Pennsylvania whose minimum wage was 16 percent less.

Many studies have been done comparing the effect of raising the minimum wage in states as divergent as California and Georgia, which have different demographics, industries, and sizes of undocumented populations. This resembles comparing, as the expression goes, apples to oranges. True, they're both fruits, but they come from different states. The Institute for Research on Labor and Employment, on the other hand, examined research covering a 20-year period that considered several hundred pairs of *adjacent* counties sharing similar demographics on different sides of state borders, but with different minimum wage levels. It found no difference in unemployment when one side had a higher minimum wage.[119]

Fact four, by not raising the minimum wage to $10.12, taxpayers will continue to subsidize the paychecks of low-wage workers below that level at large corporations like Walmart and fast-food franchises like McDonald's. A typical Walmart that employs 300 low-wage workers costs taxpayers up to $1.9 million a year because these workers' wages are low enough to qualify them for Medicaid and food stamps.[120]

Somehow, it has now become the government's role to subsidize the wages for a large corporation like Walmart, which had $17 billion in U.S. profits last year,[121] so it can increase its stock prices, executive salaries, and dividends. In fact, it costs taxpayers $1.2 billion each year in public assistance to subsidize McDonalds' minimum wage workers.[122] Raising the minimum wage to $10.12 would help stop large corporations from having the taxpayer subsidize their employees' wages, maximizing corporate profits with taxpayer dollars.

As the former Vice Chair of the Small Business Committee in Congress, I know the struggles that entrepreneurs deal with on a daily basis. But the facts show that as long as the minimum wage is not raised above 50 percent of the average hourly wage, franchises such as McDonald's won't lay off workers as they continue to make a profit. And those workers with better wages are more likely to spend their money on products and services provided by small businesses. In fact, job growth was higher in the 13 states that raised their minimum wages at the beginning of 2014 than in the 37 states that did not.[123] Still, we must ease the regulatory burden on small businesses and encourage greater access to capital so that business owners will be better-equipped to afford to pay their workers more. That's how we turn the minimum wage from a mandate into a process of mediated reform.

In the final analysis, increasing the minimum wage is about more than the facts and figures. Increasing the minimum wage is also about ensuring that a working mother who puts her daughter on the bus to elementary school in the early morning can be back there when the bus drops her off in the late afternoon. It's about allowing a father to take the extra time in the evening away from his second job to coach his son's baseball team with the local league. It's about putting the cost of a college education within reach for the full-time student working part-time after class to afford his books and board. And it's about giving dignity to the senior citizen working as a greeter at the local grocery whose retirement savings weren't enough to take her through her golden years, particularly after the devastation to so many seniors' savings during the recession. By empowering people with a floor below which their wage will not fall, our common purpose of a stronger society is deepened.

Reducing the Part-Time/Full-Time Worker Gap

Ever since the Great Recession officially ended, the monthly jobs reports have made for mostly encouraging headlines. Unemployment is down, both the service and goods-producing sectors are coming back, and more employers are looking to hire. But the rosy numbers we see each month about "new jobs created" can be deceiving if you don't bother to look deeper than the pure plus or minus. That's because many of those new jobs created are only part-time, and they are being taken by workers who used to work full-time.

In fact, of all workers who lost a full-time job during the recession and were then reemployed, about one-in-five now hold a part-time job.[124] In spring 2014, there were 7.5 million part-time workers who wanted to work full-time but couldn't because of poor business conditions or the inability to find a full-time job.[125] By summer, a jobs report showed an increase of almost 300,000 payroll jobs, but that was only because *part-time* jobs increased by over one million while *full-time* jobs fell by 700,000.[126] By the end of that summer, data indicated a record high number of *temporary* workers – almost 2 percent of the entire workforce.[127] We cannot settle for a part-time or temporary recovery to what was a full-time recession.

To help reduce the incentive to hire workers part-time instead of full-time, we should get rid of the employer mandate portion of the Affordable Care Act – which I have long advocated – so that workers can transition into the new health care marketplace where people have greater choice and lower costs. When I worked on and voted for the health reform bill that came out of the House of Representatives, the employer mandate was not based on how many workers a business employed, but on the percentage of payroll spent on health care.[128] But by the time the final version was passed, the employer mandate had changed to a penalty for employers who hired more than 50 full-time workers. The distinction based on the number of full-time workers caused a double disincentive for small businesses: don't hire more than 50 full-timers and convert as many to part-time as possible. While I continue to be a strong advocate of the Affordable Care Act, this piece of it must go.

In fact, for those of us who are committed to "patients first" health reform, removing the employer mandate is a good thing. Employers originally offered health insurance to their employees to attract better workers and reap the benefits of a larger pool of participants, minimizing risk. Prior to the health care marketplace established by the Affordable Care Act, there was no good alternative to an employer-based plan. But now that the health care marketplace is up and running there is an alternative – and it's cheaper.

As health care costs have increased over the span of many decades, employers have been moving toward high-deductible plans. As a result, from 2000 to 2010 alone, employees' share of the total cost of employer-sponsored health insurance has increased by almost 150 percent – putting yet another downward pressure on wages.[129] Similarly, over the past five years the employer contribution has been declining for all age groups.[130] So it's no surprise that today average premiums in the health care exchange are 4 percent lower than average premiums for similar employer-sponsored coverage.[131] In fact, an individual who chooses the lowest-cost plan in each state would see a 20 percent lower average premium than comparable employer-sponsored coverage.[132] And I'm proud to say that western Pennsylvania has one of the ten least expensive health insurance markets in the United States.[133] The fact is that we do not need an employer mandate with hiring disincentives – we only need to let the power of a fair market incentivize workers into the lower-cost health plans.

I am convinced that there will eventually come a time when there is no longer employer-based health care because individuals will choose among the hundreds of better-priced private plans offered on the better public market. We're already seeing that rates among the private plans competing in the public exchange are beating the premiums in employer plans, and as more people choose to purchase in the exchanges, the pool increases and rates fall even lower. And it won't just be IBM, GM, GE, and AT&T who have the benefit of a big risk pool; it will be all of America – especially after 2017 when larger employers may opt into the Small Business Health Options Program (SHOP).[134]

This isn't about socialism, it's about individual rights in the private market. This is exactly what the people want: a government ambitious enough to facilitate the choice of rugged individuals to make their own decisions, from which we all commonly benefit. Each one of us should have as many choices as possible in deciding how much to spend on health care. And because income is defined to include benefits, then by reducing the cost of insurance for individual and families through the health care exchange, employers will be better able to raise wages. By moving to larger pools and fewer mandates, we strengthen our ability to pursue a common enterprise.

A Corporate Tax Code That Keeps Companies Here

Just as elected leaders in my party score points on TV talking about the minimum wage, corporate tax evasion is a similarly popular target. This was most prominently on display at a Senate hearing in which Apple CEO Tim Cook testified about his company's use of something called "the double Irish with a Dutch sandwich" to keep Apple's tax rate under 10 percent in 2011.[135] And it's not just Apple that uses this technique – over a three-year span, Google was able to avoid more than $3 billion in taxes by reducing its overseas tax rate to just 2.4 percent and Twitter expects to reduce its tax payments by more than half. In 2010 alone, large companies' use of different variants of tax arrangements like the "Dutch sandwich" (broadly called "transfer pricing") reportedly cost the U.S. government as much as $60 billion.[136]

Wondering how these companies manage to make a double Irish with a Dutch sandwich? In one variety, a U.S. company cooks up new intellectual property, such as an innovative design or a pharmaceutical. Unlike cars or coffee tables, intellectual property is easily transported across borders. The company's first step is to create an Irish subsidiary that's a resident of a tax haven such as Bermuda. The company then licenses the right to use its design to the Irish subsidiary in Bermuda at a sharply reduced rate, even further avoiding tax on the sale of its design.

Then, in step two, the U.S. company creates two more subsidiaries: a second Irish subsidiary, located in Ireland, and a Dutch shell corporation. Ireland has the advantage of a low corporate tax rate, and it does not levy taxes on receipts from certain European Union countries.

The original Irish subsidiary in Bermuda sublicenses the design rights to the Dutch shell corporation and the second subsidiary in Ireland. This second Irish subsidiary then sends profit payments related to the use of the design to the Dutch corporation, which in turn sends these payments to the original Irish company in Bermuda. In the end, all the income resides in Bermuda, avoiding taxes, while all the expenses remain in the second Irish company, which, in addition to already enjoying a favorable tax rate in Ireland, can also write off most of the business expenses.

This not only allows the company to avoid paying U.S. taxes on the true sale value of the intellectual property – it also allows the company to avoid future taxes on royalties earned from further exploitation of the design and sales by its foreign subsidiaries to others.

If the Dutch sandwich left a bad taste in your mouth, you're not alone. At the hearing, "shocked" senators chastised Apple's CEO and other corporate executives for going to such great lengths to avoid paying their fair share of taxes. And yet, these senators seemed to forget that they are the ones who write the tax codes that so many companies use as a recipe for their Dutch sandwiches and other items on the corporate tax-avoidance menu. It's not Tim Cook's fault that the tax code allows him to shift money, jobs, and tax dollars overseas – it's the Senators who sat across from him, hooting and howling for the cameras. And because our leaders are failing to hold *themselves* accountable for our broken tax code, the menu of avoidance options just keeps growing.

Here's another tax-dodging recipe, this time for what is called an "inversion." In an inversion, a large U.S. company merges with a smaller foreign company to become subsidiaries of a new foreign holding company in a low-tax country. Although the formerly U.S. company has renounced its corporate citizenship, the company continues to do most of its business in the United States while moving its U.S. income into the foreign holding company through complex debt instruments called "earnings stripping."

At the same time, the inverted company avoids U.S. taxes when the earnings of a foreign subsidiary of the U.S. corporation are repatriated to the U.S. through dividends, or "hop scotching."[137] Over the span of the last decade, there have been almost 50 U.S. companies that decided to undergo an inversion.[138] In the coming decade, conservative estimates show that we stand to lose $20 billion in corporate tax revenue by such tax avoidance.[139]

In 2014, Walgreens was considering an inversion with Alliance Boots, a British company that moved to Switzerland a few years ago. Even though Walgreens receives a quarter of its $70 billion in annual profits directly from U.S. government programs (Medicare and Medicaid), the prospect of renouncing U.S. citizenship to save $4 billion over five years seemed appetizing.[140] Fortunately, after their intention to invert became public, Walgreens decided that economic patriotism was more important than saving a small percentage of their profits. Unfortunately, too many American companies are deciding to go the other direction, even one of our favorites – Burger King.

Here's the rub: corporate CEOs are "doing their job" and finding every possible way to use the American tax code to cut costs for their investors, while Congress is failing to do its job in writing a tax code that instead incentivizes companies to stay here at home for their constituents, creating jobs and paying their share of taxes. To determine how to do this, we need to again consider the facts.

First, our corporate tax rate is too high. Currently, our federal tax rate is 35 percent, which is the highest of all OECD nations.[141] This makes the United States an unappealing home for foreign companies and creates a temptation for our domestic companies to flee overseas, taking jobs, investment, and tax revenues with them.

Second, though, is the fact that our tax code is filled with deductions, credits, and loopholes that allow corporations to pay an effective rate of somewhere between 13 and 17 percent[142] – and even lower for large firms who can afford expensive accountants and top notch tax attorneys. A Government Accountability Office (GAO) study in 2008 found that 55 percent of large corporations had a federal tax liability of 0 percent in at least one of eight years studied.[143] In comparison, small businesses – which tend to be organized as S corporations or partnerships – pay an effective rate of about 30 percent, according to the National Federation of Independent Businesses.[144]

Third, the share of federal revenue generated by the corporate income tax has gone from 32 percent under President Dwight D. Eisenhower to just 9 percent in 2010, even as corporate profits reached all-time highs.[145] Because the corporate share dropped so dramatically, the burden is being shifted onto working families and small businesses. In 2010, payroll and individual income taxes together accounted for about 80 percent of federal tax revenues.[146]

Fourth, corporations using techniques comparable to the Dutch sandwich have been holding money overseas to avoid taxation for so long that there is now an estimated $2.1 trillion in offshore earnings that could be used here at home.[147] But instead of paying the high taxes to spend that money in America, corporations are instead incentivized to undergo inversions to access these foreign profits.

Given these facts, I support lowering the corporate rate to as low as 20 percent, but only if we also close the loopholes that these corporations are using to avoid paying taxes –

which has permitted them to pay a 13 to 17 percent rate, on average. This 20 percent tax rate is competitive globally – it is lower than the 24 percent OECD average.[148] By lowering the overall corporate tax rate, businesses will have greater flexibility for supporting wages and investments as they keep their operations here at home. But closing the loopholes is just as crucial, if not more. These companies use our roads, bridges, waterways, legal system, and law enforcement. They also use the human capital developed in our schools, vocational programs, and colleges. Our tax dollars pay for all of these things, and the unprecedented level of corporate tax avoidance means big business is getting a free lunch from the rest of us.

The next question is what to do to get that $2.1 trillion in overseas accounts invested back in our economy, but at a reasonable rate. Step one is closing the loophole that allowed all that money to amass overseas in the first place, which is called the offshore corporate income tax deferral. As I said, we should only be willing to lower the tax rate if we also get rid of the loopholes. Step two is offering these companies an incentive to bring that money back home, creating American jobs with good pay. But instead of offering a tax holiday, which was what President Bush did in 2004, we should be smarter about driving the point home to companies that they have a stake in their own tax dollars.

Here's how we do it. President Bush's tax holiday charged companies 5 percent for bringing their untaxed offshore profits back home. I propose a hybrid holiday in which companies are charged 10 percent, but are offered the option of keeping half of that amount to invest exclusively in either human capital through workforce training and retraining programs (as you will see in the next chapter, training by companies has suffered as a result of the recent recession) or another true capital investment here at home. These programs could be self-developed, in partnership with vocational schools and community colleges, or done in partnership with other corporations. That way, the taxpayers would be guaranteed to get the same amount we got in 2004 (5 percent), but corporations would also invest in creating a 21st century workforce with capital investment that fits their needs. In fact, an additional incentive should be created if the capital investment is put into small business because of the job creation that would result from such access to capital, as laid out in an earlier chapter.

Corporate tax reform shouldn't be about browbeating job creators, as my party seems to enjoy at times. It's about getting rid of the incentive to go overseas and keeping jobs here at home, which in turn creates a greater demand for workers. And because businesses will see a lower tax rate, they have the flexibility to pay competitive wages for those workers, helping in both the short term and going a long way in the medium term toward increasing the median wage. Essentially, it's about accountability. I'm willing to lower the corporate tax rate, but only if corporations are willing to see their loopholes disappear and actually pay for the benefits government provides them.

Once again, it's a "win-win:" corporations get a lower tax rate; unfair tax avoidance ends; financial capital is returned to America for investment; the workforce is trained, human capital is invested in, and small business has access to the critical "mother's milk" needed to grow – financial capital. And our nation as a whole benefits, for we truly are in this together.

Section III

RESTORING OUR WORKFORCE –
ALL HANDS ON DECK

Chapter 6

A WORKFORCE THAT KEEPS PACE WITH THE NEW ECONOMY

Y ou really appreciate the value of a trained workforce when you live on an aircraft carrier – a floating airfield powered by a nuclear reactor – run by sailors with an average age of 19-and-a-half. On my first ship when I entered the Navy during the Vietnam War era, only one of my five Senior and Chief Petty Officers had a high school degree. By the time I commanded an aircraft carrier battle group decades later, you weren't going to be able to attain the level of Senior Chief Petty Officer without an associate's degree, usually in technology, because that's what the job demanded. That's why, as I said in the first chapter, we provided each sailor a career of training, education, and retraining so that our overall military readiness would have their full contribution as each sailor would have the opportunity to achieve individually the skills he or she valued as their personal role.

Just as the Navy invested in me by sending me to Harvard to get a masters degree and a Ph.D., a fire control technician would first go to school for basic engineering maintenance, a few years later be further trained on repairing the sophisticated radar systems, and then years after that going for additional schooling and training for the entire fire control system and the electronic intricacies of other parts of the ship.

Even for our Navy's cooks, this process holds true. We send our cooks to the Culinary Specialist "A" School for a training program in partnership with the American Culinary Federation that issues sailors a nationally-recognized certificate. A sailor might start his career flipping burgers as a "fast cook culinary professional" and after 20 to 30 years of training become a certified 5-star master chef with an ACF Executive Chef certification and a Bachelors degree in Culinary Arts.

The Navy built these training rungs on our career ladder – and invested in them – not because we're run by socialists but because we need all hands on deck. We need skilled workers at all levels of operation. The same can be said of the 21st century U.S. economy.

Human Capital is Just as Important as Financial Capital

As globalization and technology rapidly accelerate, the American worker needs to be increasingly agile just to keep up. Gone are the days of learning a skill on the job and honing that talent until retirement. If we are going to be competitive, the 21st century worker will need life-long training and retraining as entire sectors of the economy are reinvented and renewed. As the baby boomers retire, this next generation of workers needs to have the skills to pick up where the boomers left off and keep carrying the torch. As high-tech machinery replaces skilled workers on factory floors, those same workers need new skills to build and keep the machinery running and to invent the next generation – especially in the new green manufacturing sector.

Even as our economy is recovering and unemployment has decreased, employers are experiencing holes in hiring because of a widening skills gap. For instance, 7,000 business leaders recently cited the decline in skilled labor as undermining American competitiveness.[149] Similarly, one-third of small business owners said they had unfilled job openings because they couldn't identify qualified applicants.[150] So while we must do more to make sure our entrepreneurs have access to *financial* capital, as I've discussed before, business owners' ability to innovate will be stunted unless we also ensure access to *human* capital.

Unfortunately, U.S. spending on labor training has been decreasing since 1979 and is now – at one-tenth of one percent of GDP – the lowest among high-income, developed economies.[151] The private sector has also let investment in training programs fall by the wayside in order to stay afloat in the wake of the recession. A recent MIT study found that manufacturers' spending on training has been flat for the last five years, and research from Deloitte, a research and consulting firm, shows that the percentage of manufacturers' training and development staff fell by almost half from 2006 to 2013.[152] Similarly, apprentice programs registered with the Labor Department have fallen from 33,000 in 2002 to 21,000 in 2012.[153]

If policymakers do nothing in response, the skills gap is only going to widen. It is estimated that, by 2022, the U.S. will need 11 million more workers with education and training beyond high school, 40 percent of which includes workers with postsecondary vocational certificates, college credits, or associate's degrees.[154] Some economists estimate that close to half of all U.S. jobs in the coming years will require more than high school but less than four years of college – that means associate degrees, occupational certificates, industry certifications, and apprenticeships.[155] To meet this challenge, however, the answer isn't just to have the government spend more money.

In fact, what's worse than our nation's failure to invest sufficiently in workforce development is the abject failure of the programs in which we have invested. With the Government Accountability Office (GAO) concluding in 2011 that 47 skills-based training programs – almost all overlapping and spread across nine different government agencies – lack oversight and waste tax dollars,[156] why should we invest in them? How can we justify spending $18 billion on those 47 different programs when just five of them had conducted an effectiveness study in the previous five years to measure their impact and the return on our investment?[157] Where's the accountability?

It took the government a full three years after the release of the GAO report to reform our training programs. The resulting response, culminating in The Workforce Innovation and Opportunity Act, made a number of much-needed reforms. The Act, for instance, eliminates 15 overlapping and wasteful programs, creates a single system to measure outcomes, institutes greater local control, increases support for pay-for-performance contracts, and prioritizes programs that lead to nationally recognized credentials.[158][159]

Unfortunately, we still have a long way to go, as reports of waste remain too pervasive for comfort in the news. For example, money had reportedly gone to training programs at fraudulent for-profit colleges like Corinthian Colleges Inc., which had been the longtime subject of an Education Department investigation.[160] Other institutions are advertising false job-placement numbers to attract government grants for those who are out of work.[161]

Rethinking Retraining

Making our existing training programs effective and eliminating the ones considered wasteful are, of course, good starting points – but that's not nearly enough. For the truth is that we need to fundamentally rethink how we retrain and prepare our workforce for the new, highly competitive, and globalized economy. Our first step should be to increase accountability for results by assessing what has already been proven to work so we know where to direct our precious resources. Most of the training programs that show measurable success are run by state and local agencies – not the federal government – with strong private sector involvement. They succeeded because these programs are organized to serve the needs of their local labor market conditions and populations.

Knowing all this, the federal government should focus more of its efforts on potentially promising options at the local and state levels – as a helpful facilitator for, but not driver of, good programs – and provide them with the much needed resources and support.

Let me give you one example of what a successful, locally-driven program could look like. In 2013, I spoke at the graduation ceremony for ITWorks, a private non-profit that provides free training in information technology (IT) to young adults in Philadelphia. The city ranks fourth in the nation for the total number of young adults not in school, not employed full-time, and without a postsecondary degree. But by tapping into trapped populations through training, the graduates I met were equipped with the tools to compete in today's economy. ITWorks' training program is successful because it partners with local companies to develop industry-specific curriculum. These same companies provide equipment for the program so that the training students receive is directly relevant and applicable to the everyday experiences and needs of local industries.

After completing the training program, students at ITWorks are placed into tech-related internships at area corporations – corporations that already have a vested interest in the students because it was their very equipment and curriculum on which the students were trained. After completing the internship, most students transition into full-time workers, equipped with skills, experience, a professional IT certification, and the ability to move up the company ladder.

Successful private industry models exist across the country. In recent years, Cascade Engineering paired with Burger King to create a program giving low-skilled job seekers with little to no experience a chance to train for a better job.[162] Job-seekers worked at Burger King for six to 12 months while participating in skill development training, and employees who proved their perseverance became eligible to work at Cascade Engineering in better-paying jobs. For both companies, it was a mutually beneficial undertaking: Burger King gained because it recruited committed employees and Cascade Engineering had a pool of employees who had work skills, training, and proven backgrounds as determined goal seekers.

In Texas, the "Capital IDEA" program helped low-skilled workers gain employment in high-growth sectors. Participants increased earnings by as much as $3,100 seven years after enrollment, and each dollar invested in the program gave a return of $1.65 over 10 years to taxpayers.[163] In Minnesota, the "Twin Cities RISE!" program originally received most of its money from donations, but now has a performance contract from the state. Over 80 percent of participants who find jobs after the seven month training program stay in those jobs for over a year. According to the Minneapolis Federal Reserve, every $1 invested in Twin Cities RISE! yields $7 for the taxpayers.[164]

On balance, in my travels and conversations with people across Pennsylvania and the nation about the ways in which we run training programs, I have learned that the private sector – not government directly, but at times as a facilitator – is best suited to help the determined individuals in the workforce who are trying to move up. While it is refreshing to see Congress and the President inching closer to local management and performance-based contracts, government should instead be trying to get out of the way and transition to the role of facilitator.

To determine what that would look like, we must look at the facts. Today, we have businesses in need of skilled workers, and workers in need of training while industries have reduced their training budgets in recent years. We certainly do not want to have a national shortage of skilled workers – which would be a detriment to us all. The government has some role to play in response to all this, to be sure, but given its relatively poor track record of focusing on the right programs and ensuring their effectiveness, it could define its role as facilitator and convener, matching private sector talents with the right initiatives in the right communities, with appropriate resources.

Private industry and government – as needed to facilitate – can, in fact, work together to secure more money for job training through new, experimental programs. A prime example of this is a federal program that sells "Workplace Development Performance Bonds" to private sector investors.[165]

A variation of this type of bond-selling program to raise funds for job training already exists in Minnesota's Human Capital Performance Bond. The city government would enter into contracts with training and retraining program providers, compensating them based on performance evaluation metrics. The government would raise the money to pay for these providers by selling bonds to private sector investors. This type of arrangement saves the government time and money, puts development programs in the hands of proven, successful providers, allows for the raising of funds through private investors – and, above all, ensures that our prime target for doing all this, the workers, get the valuable job training and retraining that they need to survive, compete, and succeed in this global economy.[166]

And it is in this type of arrangement where we can see, first hand, how government power can be a positive force for advancing our workers' well-being – and our nation's long-term, common good – instead of being a passive broker of wasteful projects without being forced to face any trace of accountability. There is much more, of course, that we can do for our workforce including reforms to education, student debt, and immigration. I will address these in coming chapters.

Chapter 7

A Health Security Strategy

At four years old, my daughter Alex was diagnosed with aggressive brain cancer and given a single-digit chance of survival. My wife, daughter, and I fought hard, and Alex eventually overcame the odds and beat this terrible illness. Thanks to the grace of God, Alex was given the courage to endure several operations and the ravages of high-dose chemotherapy and radiation. It is thanks to the high-quality TRICARE health coverage I received as a Navy sailor that Alex was given the chance to use that courage and beat cancer, armed with the best treatments available.

I will never forget during our time in Children's Hospital hearing the anguish of another family on the other side of the curtain – a family that did not have access to health coverage. Their child, a young boy maybe two years younger than Alex, faced a similar prognosis, but their options to treat his acute leukemia were severely limited because they did not have health coverage. As my wife Susan and I focused on keeping our daughter entertained and upbeat (really, she did that for us) as she underwent her treatment, we couldn't help but hear in that small room the other family talking about the limited options that were available to their son. Susan and I kept exchanging glances, both thinking, "Yes, our family has a serious hurdle in front of us, but at least we have health care coverage."

Access to health care is a deeply personal issue for me, not an abstract political discussion. It is the reason why I ran for Congress – to make sure every American has access to the same level of care that saved my daughter's life. You gave me TRICARE in the military and paid for my family to have access to quality health care; I ran for office to pay you back for what I owed you. Yes, I served my country along with my family; but my country was there for us when we needed it. My payback tour was to run for Congress so that the care my daughter received is the care that everyone could have.

In the military, we give everybody health care not because we are liberals, but because it pays great dividends to our nation. Seal Team 6 isn't ready to go when one of their members has an abscessed tooth that has been left untreated or not prevented. The unit as a whole cannot be focused on the mission if even one of them is worrying about the family being covered back home. Health care is a significant part of military readiness, and without it there would be a serious long-term degradation of our overall readiness – as the very first U.S. Congress realized in mandating a health care system for American merchant sailors.

Just as we need a productive warrior force to carry out our national defense mission, our national workforce must be equally able to carry out our economic mission. To be productive and focused, the rugged individuals in our economy need health security so that our country can remain competitive and agile in the changing economy. We need all hands on deck, and all hands need to be healthy to be productive.

An Unhealthy Debate

When I was first elected to Congress in 2006, the Democratic House leadership wanted to put me on the House Intelligence Committee because of my national security experience running the Navy's anti-terrorism unit and because I served on President Clinton's National Security Council. Yes, I wanted to serve (and did) on the Armed Services Committee to bring my experience and expertise to bear on our nation's foreign and military policies. But I also wanted to be on the Health, Employment, Labor, and Pensions (HELP) Subcommittee (a key part of the Education Committee) because my experience in the military taught me that while our armed services can keep us safe, our strength as a nation begins at home and comes from the strength of our working families – their jobs, health, and education.

I saw this in the youth who came into our military, which is why I was also on the full Education Committee and asked to have a waiver to be on a third committee – the Small Business Committee, where I was Vice Chairman. But because I knew that health care legislation would have to come through HELP, I knew that was where I most had to be. And I had that opportunity to improve our nation's health security when the health care overhaul began in Congress.

Our efforts would ultimately produce a far better health security for our nation and its people, but unfortunately, given Congress' dysfunction, the process and debate fell short of what we owed the American people. Deal-making took precedence over crafting the best policy. Too much was done behind closed doors. Even the way that the final legislation arrived at the President's desk was flawed: the House spent the summer of 2009 crafting bills that we sent over to the Senate, by fall the Senate threw out parts of that legislation and inserted in places its own proposals as an amendment to a wholly unrelated bill about armed service members' home ownership taxes; we then spent the entire winter negotiating parts of the overall package with the White House, and eventually Leadership used the reconciliation process in the Budget Control Act to pass the final Patient Protection and Affordable Care Act, which the President signed in March 2010.

In other words, our process was impacted too much by special interests, done too much in the dark with too little bipartisanship, and relied too heavily on obscure legislative maneuvers.

On the other side, there were false claims – even notably, the outrageous claim of "death panels" – that further betrayed the integrity and seriousness that our democratic process required. Rather than honest and open debate, too many favored a campaign of deliberate misinformation and the politics of division, allowing fear to fracture the unity that binds us as Americans in order to score political points. Likewise, the media too often neglected its role as a fair arbiter of information for the American people in order, it seemed at times, to score higher ratings points.

Our nation was sent into the shoal water where we almost ran aground, resulting in a loss of faith in our leadership and unnecessary uncertainty about the direction of our proposed solutions and reforms.

As our national dialogue on health care access became increasingly poisonous, many of my fellow members of Congress cancelled appearances at public forums for fear of confrontation. I held health care town halls across my district, then scheduled hour-or-more-long meetings in all of Pennsylvania's 67 counties as I began to run for Senate, and went everywhere I could – even eagerly on FOX News – to answer questions and make the case for reform. As many remember, the debate over health care during that summer was a difficult one – with members across the country being shouted down by angry and anxious constituents, scenes that often found their way to being played endlessly on cable news channels. Even so, a public servant owes it to one's constituents to always face their questions, listen, and provide answers honestly and candidly.

At the time, those of us in public office needed to be especially responsive to the anxiety that Americans felt during a savage recession. And, naturally, whenever great policy changes are proposed, people are, rightly, often uncertain. As members of Congress, it is our job to provide honest, fact-based answers that satisfy our people. The debates in our democracy must be founded on the conviction that while we may have differing ideas, we all want what is best for America.

Restoring Trust and Keeping Promises

Despite the imperfect process and the toxic debate, the Affordable Care Act (ACA) has taken critical steps toward fair access to quality care and lower costs through private market mechanisms. No longer are life-and-death decisions made by insurance bureaucrats instead of families and doctors. Never again will insurance companies be permitted to deny or drop customers like my daughter who have "pre-existing conditions." The Medicare donut hole that forced seniors to pay exorbitant drug costs is closed. Price discrimination against women and the elderly is prohibited. Young people can stay on their parents' insurance until age 26. Free preventive exams to catch illness early are required for every plan, as is prenatal care for pregnant women. All this and more, while decreasing the national debt and cutting in half the growth of America's health care costs.

These immediate changes were crucial reforms for our system, and marked the beginning steps in our promise to protect patients and make health care more affordable. Years later, after further implementation, it is even clearer that we are keeping our promise of reigning in health care costs:

- In the four years since the ACA was passed, the per capita cost of health care rose at half the rate of the preceding 8 years, at 3 percent compared to over 6 percent.[167] That's the slowest cost increase in 50 years,[168] and a sign that the cost curve is finally bending.
- Average premiums in the health care exchanges are 4 percent lower than average premiums for similar employer-sponsored coverage.[169] As more people choose amongst the cheaper plans in the marketplace, the prices will go down even further. For 2015, because more people are in the marketplace to drive down costs, more than 7 in 10 marketplace enrollees had lower-premium plans available at the same category of coverage.[170]
- Because premiums on the exchange are estimated to be 15 percent lower in 2016 than originally expected in 2010, the CBO estimates the health care expansion will result in government savings of an extra $100 billion over the next decade.[171] That means more money to save or to invest elsewhere.

- Before reform, double-digit annual increases in premiums were the norm. Now, the national average premium increase for 2015 is estimated to have fallen to 7.5 percent.[172] There's still work to be done – that 7.5 percent average spans a 23 percent rate cut through a 36 percent rate hike – but the overall numbers show we're moving in the right direction.[173][174]

- With more and more private insurers selling health coverage on the exchanges – a 25 percent increase for the 2015 enrollment period – increased price competition can only mean more competitive prices.[175] In fact, a 44-state analysis found that the number of new marketplace insurers was five times greater than insurers exiting the market, creating more choice for individual consumers and new opportunities for issuers with lower, competitive pricing.[176]

- In the marketplaces set up for small businesses, plans offered through the Small Business Health Options Program (SHOP) exchanges have premiums 7 percent less expensive than plans sold off the health care marketplace.[177] That's because small employers like a local landscaping company can now pool together in the SHOP marketplace to gain the efficiency of a large group market like IBM.

The ACA has also led to various other savings throughout the health care system that are lowering costs to consumers:

- Through rebates and discounts to close the "donut hole" gap in Medicare prescription drug coverage, over 8 million seniors and people with disabilities have saved $12 billion since 2010 – an average of $1,500 per person.[178] For seniors on a fixed income, every dollar of these extra savings has meaning.

- In 2014, almost 7 million people will have received $330 million in "MLR" rebates, a value of about $80 per family.[179] The "medical loss ratio" (MLR) portion of the ACA requires insurance companies to spend at least 80 percent of health care premiums on medical care, which is meant to lower spending on salaries and bonuses. If an insurance company fails to meet the MLR, they must provide customers with refunds. In 2013, almost $500 million in rebates were returned to consumers.[180]

- The Department of Health and Human Services estimates that consumers would have spent almost $4 billion extra dollars on premiums in 2013 if health insurance companies kept the 2011 ratio of premiums versus cost of care.[181] That means more money in everyone's pocket to spend, save, and invest.

Medicare has also been further strengthened by the Affordable Care Act, keeping our promise to today's seniors and the disabled, while extending that promise further into the future:

- The ACA has also added 13 years to the life of the Medicare trust fund, which will now be solvent through 2030 compared to the 2017 estimate before the ACA was passed.[182]

- Medicare has a new lease on life because the ACA has kept costs down. For example, even though coverage under Medicare Part A's hospital insurance program was extended to an extra 1 million people in 2013, the program spent *less* than it did in 2012.[183] In fact, because hospitals are now incentivized to avoid readmitting patients, 150,000 fewer patients were readmitted in 2012 and 2013.[184]

- At the same time, the growth in premiums charged to beneficiaries of Medicare Part B has slowed to almost zero percent – spending rose by just $1 per beneficiary in 2013[185] – meaning that for the third straight year,[186] the $105 average premium would remain almost exactly the same.[187]

- The cost of avoidable hospital readmissions – estimated to cost Medicare $17 billion annually – is decreasing as the ACA's fines on hospitals with excessive readmission rates incentivize them to focus on post-discharge health.[188]

- And similarly, because of incentives to keep patients healthier (like financial penalties for high readmission rates), hospital errors have dropped 17 percent since 2010 – saving 50,000 lives and $12 billion to the health care system.[189]

Most importantly, more people are insured than ever before because of health care reform, while lowering health care costs:

- Data shows that 6 in 10 people who bought their own health insurance through exchanges set up through the ACA were previously uninsured.[190] Reducing the number of uninsured Americans is crucial because the cost to our economy of underinsurance and the uninsured is estimated by the Institute of Medicine to be between $65 and $130 billion annually.[191]

- According to estimates from Gallup, the Urban Institute, and RAND Corp., somewhere between 8 million and 11 million people gained coverage from the end of summer 2013 through the end of spring 2014,[192] far surpassing CBO enrollment forecasts.[193]
- As a result, the uninsured rate fell from about 20 percent to about 14 percent.[194]
- That means that roughly 1 of 4 people who were uninsured before the first enrollment period now have coverage, with untapped potential still remaining.[195] Every enrollment period will bring us closer to universal coverage, increasing the pool along the way, and resulting in a more productive workforce and healthier families.

I believe that the Affordable Care Act will go down in history as an example of what America does best: increasing the freedom of the people to make their own decisions so that we all might benefit in our common enterprise. In choosing to enter health care exchanges, each person can choose the plan that works best for them, not for their employer, widening the pool and decreasing the common cost for us all. In choosing to participate in free preventative care, each person reduces the chance of unexpected catastrophic illness, keeping themselves in good health and keeping our future expenses lower. And in choosing affordable coverage instead of relying on the emergency room, our shared burden is lessened. Our nation of rugged individuals will be healthier and more financially secure, more productive and ready to contribute to our economy, and freer to determine their own fate and that of their family.

Expect What You Inspect

I learned in the Navy to expect what you inspect. A good captain gets off the bridge wing and goes down to the mess decks and engine rooms and walks around everywhere – he or she knows what's happening on his or her ship. As much as I strongly support the Affordable Care Act, there was a lack of accountable leadership in implementing it. The administration exhibited poor execution and failed to make sure that promises were kept. As a result, the biggest debt in the nation – which is not budget deficit but the trust deficit – was again severely impacted. In a democracy, a government that loses the faith of the people loses everything.

From the beginning, the White House failed to get sufficiently involved in writing the bill aside from providing Congress with a vague "set of eight principles" in February of 2009. After a spring, summer, and fall of competition among congressmen, senators, lobbyists, special interests, different committees, different bills, and different directions, all hell had broken loose. Instead of sitting on the sidelines so long, the Chief Executive should have set the benchmarks he wanted to be accountable for in the establishment of the new health care policy.

Then, after the ACA finally passed, the Health and Human Services Secretary was permitted to write administrative rules that broke our promise to the American people of "if you like your plan, you can keep it." The ACA provided for "grandfathering" in old plans that didn't provide essential health benefits, so long as there were no "significant changes" in deductibles, co-payments, or benefits. Unfortunately, the Administration then defined "significant changes" in such a narrow way that people could not keep the plan they already liked. After 2010, as I began teaching, I watched as Congress did not provide oversight of the administration's actions and as a result they could only expect what they *did not* inspect.

Then there's the website. Someone said it best: if our government could execute a plan to beat Germany and Japan in World War II, how could it not roll out a website in four years? Rather than saying "I take full responsibility for making sure it gets fixed", what we need our public officials to say is "I am accountable for it being broken." A good captain must know what is happening below deck, and is personally accountable for the errors of those under his command.

That said, I believe the ACA is a vast improvement on our nation's health care system for the reasons I described above and more. But I also believe that restoring the trust deficit must be the major priority for our leaders. The positive results thus far do go a long way toward rebuilding that trust. Yet what we must do now is focus our efforts on making sure that health reform does continue to work for working families – and that public officials be willing to be accountable that it does. I have already said in a previous chapter that we need to get rid of the employer mandate because of its part-time versus full-time employment incentive, but there are many additional, constructive steps we must take to build a better system. Our health security depends on it – so does our faith in our democracy and its public servants.

Brokering a Better Bargain

An immediate step we must take is empowering individuals to purchase the medication they need at a price they can afford. Too often, ailing Americans are skipping prescription refills or cutting pills in half because they can't afford the cost of keeping healthy. And while the ACA has gone a long way in stabilizing and lowering costs, each person should be able to pursue the lowest possible price for safe prescription medication. That's why I support allowing individuals to import cheaper drugs from Canada (where our own pharmaceutical firms often sell the same drug for a significantly lower price), so long as the pharmacies are approved and the safety standards of the pharmaceutical chains – from manufacturing to customer – are the same as in the United States.

This is a common sense solution, and it has already been proven successful. Maine has permitted citizens to reimport drugs from Canada for close to a decade now, first permitting residents over the age of 62 and disabled residents to import needed drugs in 2005.[196] City employees in Portland, Maine, began buying Canadian drugs in 2006.[197] As a result, they have reaped the benefits of paying, for example, $113 for a month's prescription of Cymbalta instead of $149; $29 for Nasonex instead of $105; an overall average of $600 per person per year on pharmaceuticals instead of $1,000.[198][199]

I understand that pharmaceutical companies make the case that they need to generate significant profits to pay for the crucial research and development that goes into creating innovative new drugs. That is a valid argument I would be willing to accept – if the same companies didn't spend $27 billion a year on marketing their drugs.[200] That's enough to buy 6,750 different Super Bowl ads.[201] As a result of these companies dumping so much money into advertising, the cost to American consumers is inflated, even while our tax dollars subsidize the research and development tax incentives that the same pharmaceutical companies use to further defray their costs.

In 2009, we tried to include drug reimportation into the health care overhaul, but the Administration struck reimportation from the reform agenda in exchange for the support of pharmaceutical companies in the overall reform.[202] Instead of brokering political deals, we should allow individuals to broker their own deals with safe, established providers so that we all benefit from lower health care spending, greater price competition among providers, and more money to spend in other sectors of the economy.

For similar reasons, we should allow Medicare to bargain directly with drug-makers – as Medicaid and the Department of Veterans Affairs already do. Currently, federal law prohibits Medicare from negotiating directly with pharmaceutical companies for cheaper drug prices. Only private insurers that offer drug insurance under Medicare can engage in such negotiations. The Congressional Budget Office estimates that negotiating rebates would produce savings of $123 billion from 2015 to 2023.[203]

For example, a data analysis of the lowest price obtained by Medicare Part D prescription drug plans for the generic form of Lasix compared to the price obtained by the VA after negotiating with the pharmaceutical company was a difference of almost 65 percent.[204] For Lipitor, the difference was almost 30 percent. How wrong that is, and how unaccountable our elected officials are to permit that inequity and waste of our resources.

This potential for taxpayer savings might sound familiar if you followed the health care debate closely – the bill we passed in the House would have required the Health and Human Services Secretary to negotiate directly with manufacturers starting in 2011 for drugs in Medicare Part D plans.[205] But unfortunately, that part of our bill didn't make it into the final health care legislation because the Executive Branch gave in to the pharmaceutical lobby's demands in exchange for their political support of a final package.[206] We need to increase our common bargaining power so that we each spend less money on prescription drugs, empowering each of us to make more of our own health decisions, and redirect our dollars where we want them.

Health care doesn't have to be a conflict between patients who need treatment and drug companies that want to create more cures. If the pharmaceutical industry needs to spend more money on R&D, we can provide for that through tax incentives – or other appropriate means such as safely fast-tracking key drugs through the Federal Drug Administration's approval process – instead of allowing it to charge exorbitant prices and put those profits toward TV ads.

Industry Incentives – What Works, What to Watch, and Where to Make Changes

So much of what is working under the ACA is based on using a change in incentives to revolutionize the health care industry. Accountable Care Organizations (ACOs) – which consist of doctors, nurses, and other health care professionals who come together voluntarily to provide more efficient and less duplicative care for Medicare patients – have perhaps the most potential to cut overall health care costs while providing a higher standard of care. Under the traditional fee-for-service model, doctors and hospitals have the financial incentive to perform as many tests and procedures as possible on a patient, without care for reasonable costs or the integrated quality of care for patient's health.

The new ACOs, however, are incentivized to provide *quality* care, not a *quantity* of care. Each ACO is a network of doctors and hospitals that join together to coordinate care for thousands of Medicare patients and patients in the commercial market, and receive bonuses for keeping costs down and meeting medical quality benchmarks for their patients. The incentive switches from providing as many services as possible to preventing as much illness as possible.

In the first year that groups of doctors and hospitals participated in Medicare ACO programs, the 137 ACOs involved saved a total of $380 million, of which about $130 million of the savings was put back into the Medicare Trust Fund and the rest went to the ACOs that met the savings levels and quality benchmarks.[207] By the beginning of 2013, there were 428 ACOs in 49 states[208] serving an estimated 14 percent of the U.S. population.[209] Their growth is a testament to the success of the new incentives: patients get quality care for less, doctors get a bonus based on performance outcome instead of the number of patient tests taken, and the taxpayer sees that the savings make Medicare more solvent.

As more ACOs are formed and coordinated care is refined, this bargain will only get better. But we have to be careful that we do not create a scenario down the road where ACOs become so integrated that they actually reduce competition, causing higher prices and a decreased quality of care. Incentives can be tricky – you have to promote growth without creating a leviathan. Currently, the Federal Trade Commission and the Department of Justice have laid out guidelines for ACOs to stay within the bounds of anti-trust laws.[210] While these guidelines are workable right now, in the infancy of the health reform law, Congress needs to remain constantly vigilant that we don't eventually see a system of regional ACO monopolies where anti-competition incentives outweigh quality care bonuses.

Similarly, ACOs have been given a special waiver for certain services from the federal physician self-referral law that prohibits physicians from referring Medicare or Medicaid patients to entities in which the physician has a financial interest. The physician self-referral rule is a crucial component of our fee-for-service model – a doctor who makes money each time he sends a patient for a particular test is incentivized to conduct unnecessary testing, and the taxpayer foots the fee for the extra "services." For example, a Government Accountability Office study found that Medicare and Medicaid physicians who began self-referring MRI and CT scans in 2009 increased referrals on average by 67 percent in 2010 compared to 2008.[211]

ACOs, however, have been given a waiver from the physician self-referral law because of the nature of referrals among coordinated physician and hospital groups for a share in the savings from *fewer* unnecessary tests and procedures.[212] ACOs are incentivized to reduce expenditures, not rack up testing bills. As ACOs continue to grow and our national health care model continues to shift from fee-for-service to fee-for-outcome, we must monitor the changing incentives for physicians to self-refer. The entire self-referral statute is based on a system of incentives that is rapidly disappearing. We need to make sure our anti-waste laws adapt to this changing environment.

One incentive we need to reverse right now is the "pay-for-delay" scheme that both brand name and generic pharmaceutical companies use to extort money from each other and pass the bill on to consumers. Under current law, a brand name pharmaceutical company can enter into a patent litigation settlement agreement with a generic company and pay the generic brand to delay their competing product from entering the market because the original patent by the brand name company is expiring. Both companies win – the brand name company gets to continue to charge prices as much as 90 percent higher than a generic product would cost, and the generic brand company gets paid for doing nothing.

Consumers, all the while, are stuck paying higher prices for the medicines they need, and taxpayers are stuck footing a higher bill for the drug subsidies in our social programs. In fact, the Federal Trade Commission estimates that "pay for delay" deals cost consumers and taxpayers $3.5 billion every year[213] and delay generic entry into the market by an average of 17 months.[214] In 2011, there were an estimated 28 "pay for delay" deals involving 25 different brand name products with annual U.S. sales of close to $10 billion.[215] Congress needs to act immediately to prohibit brand name pharmaceutical companies from entering these settlement agreements with their generic competitors.

This is a step by we the people to ensure fairness in the private market when a patent has expired and a "monopoly" exists for a particular brand drug, which supports the fundamental American belief that a healthy, competitive business environment creates more innovation and more consumer choice. Individuals need more choices, not fewer. By using the power of government – We the People – to stop anticompetitive practices, we all benefit from lower costs and wider access.

All Healthy Hands on Deck

For our nation, one of the key responsibilities for policymakers in the 21st century is to make America a competitive country, able to go head-to-head with any other country in the world. In a global economy, where money, talents, and investments can go just about anywhere, we need to ensure that the United States can offer an even more attractive environment for businesses and workers to excel. By pushing forward with much needed reforms in the health care realm, we can make our system more efficient, lower costs and thereby benefit companies and consumers alike, and empower Americans with a peace of mind so that they can assert themselves fully and confidently in this new but too often uncertain economic landscape, knowing that they are never just one illness away from facing bankruptcy. In short, we need all hands to be able and healthy to stay on deck and secure prosperity for all Americans in the decades to come.

Chapter 8

UNTAPPED ASSETS IN THE AMERICAN WORKFORCE

The preceding chapters in this section have addressed what we must do to strengthen the individuals already in our workforce so that we all benefit from a more productive and vibrant economy. This chapter looks at certain segments of untapped human resources and the ways in which they can augment our national endeavor to bring more able hands fully on deck in order to fully fire up the engine of our economic ship of state. In the paragraphs to follow, I want to look at two of such subsets of our working population: new immigrants and those who have served time in our correction system.

Obviously, they are very different from each other, but both could certainly make greater contributions in their respective ways to the American economy if they were more fully integrated and utilized in our job market. How can we more effectively weave new Americans into the fabric of our nation's economy? And how can we help those – and better benefit America – who have already repaid society for the wrongs that they have committed reenter the nation's job market as productive, tax-paying citizens?

These ideas and questions may not be agreeable to some, but in my view they are also uniquely American.

The mighty woman who, with torch in hand, makes her proud presence known in New York Harbor has for over a century welcomed those who yearned to breathe free – including my father, the best man I ever knew. More than most symbols, Lady Liberty represents our society's commitment to granting all Americans a second chance and limitless opportunity – whether for those who had the courage to sever previous ties in order to start new lives in a new land, or for those who, stuck in a cycle of poverty and imprisonment, simply want to find a path to more productive lives after having erred.

Smarter Immigration for More Innovation

As the son of a man who left his homeland and arrived in America to search for a better life for himself and his family, I believe that our immigrant heritage adds richness to our country's storied history and much promise to our collective future. All immigrants, by definition, are rugged individuals who came to America to work hard, provide for their family, and ensure that their children have the opportunity for better lives and make even greater contributions to their new country. Throughout our nation's history, our common enterprise has benefitted greatly from the contributions of new comers – many of them arrived in this country with nothing, and yet through hard work managed to allow their children to become doctors, scientists, journalists, teachers, engineers, and even three-star admirals. Immigrants have been part of the American success story in every field; in fact, 40 percent of Forbes 500 companies were founded by immigrants or children of immigrants.[216]

For decades now, our immigration system has been broken and in dire need of reform. Congress' failure to pass comprehensive reforms of the immigration system is harming our nation – limiting our law enforcement's ability to strengthen border security; turning away skilled workers and inventors from our shores; preventing family reunifications and, in some cases, tearing children and parents apart; and, frankly, failing to properly address the challenges relating to illegal immigration. To most Americans, none of these are partisan concerns, and, for the good of our country, both parties should be able to find non-controversial and sensible solutions. But instead of finding policy fixes that most people could support, our leaders have sought out the extremes: the far right wants to round up and deport each and every illegal immigrant in every corner of the country, while the far left wants to grant instant amnesty to all and register 12 million new and, seemingly, Democratic voters.

Both of these approaches are wrong. It is neither practical nor consistent with our ideals to think that we can find 12 million undocumented immigrants, rip them away from their children (which estimates suggest to be around four million) who were born here and therefore are citizens, and ship them away. Similarly, any path to naturalization for those who are here illegally should include stringent requirements: significant fines for having violated immigration laws, repayments of any back taxes, criminal background checks, proof of employment, and the ability to pass a basic English language test. If you want to contribute to our common enterprise, then you will need to prove it.

Additionally, we need to secure our southern border. When I headed the Navy's anti-terrorism unit, I saw the details on the ways in which terrorists were involved in the South American narcotics trade. That's why, to me, border security isn't just about illegal immigration – it is also a serious matter of national security. That said, when I argue for a more secure border, I am not advocating for the building of a prison-style wall across the entire border with guard towers every half-mile. Yes, of course, we need secure, modern fences and where appropriate border patrols; but we also need smart measures, such as advanced unmanned vehicles and motion detectors, to secure our borders and prevent illegal immigrants as well as drug smugglers and terrorists from entering our country.

Unmanned aerial vehicles, in particular, are able to fly for 24 hours and have the ability to identify people on the ground and send resources to intercept them. And while some are already in use, they are not adequate either in number or in operational capacity; nor are they properly maintained or integrated with other sophisticated or more traditional assets. We must invest in such technologies to help produce the results we need in our border security efforts.

In the legislative realm, I support the bipartisan comprehensive immigration reform bill that passed the Senate in 2013. It is a bill that respects our immigrant heritage, provides for our security, and creates a tough but fair path to citizenship for undocumented immigrants. While 14 Senate Republicans, including John McCain, Lindsey Graham, and Marco Rubio voted in favor of the bill, the Speaker of the House refused to take any action. The longer that Congress fails to take action, the more the crisis balloons. Our leaders need to hold themselves accountable for the consequences of their inaction.

But immigration reform isn't just about bringing a large part of our workforce out of the shadows and onto the tax rolls, it's about making sure that the process through which people legally come into the country is laser-focused on bringing in the best and the brightest – especially in STEM (science, technology, education, and mathematics) areas where our domestic labor supply needs to be constantly renourished to meet changing market demand.

Currently, even though there are almost four unemployed workers for every one job listing, there are two STEM job listings per unemployed worker.[217] Expected job growth in STEM fields will grow at twice the rate of non-STEM fields by 2018; 75 percent of the fastest growing occupations require math and science education.[218] In the medium- to long-term, this means we have to better prepare our students for the changing economy (more on that later). In the short term, we need to do everything we can to make sure America attracts and retains rugged innovators the world over. To do this, we need to update our visa system.

The Senate's stalled immigration bill would have modestly increased the cap on visas given to immigrants with specialized knowledge while, at the same time, eliminated the "diversity lottery" visa and visas for siblings.[219] Currently, two-thirds of immigration visas go to family members while many skilled immigrants are left looking for other opportunities. While our immigration system must always endeavor to preserve the immediate family unit, our system should also have the appropriate priority of brains over more-distant blood.

But rather than just increasing the raw number of specialty occupation visas, we should have legislation that exempts STEM workers from counting toward the H-1B visa cap, and create an expedited path to full citizenship for foreign born students who have earned advanced STEM degrees at American universities. That way, we retain the flexibility of the specialty worker program while providing employers the agility to help fill the empty STEM slots that the new economy needs most.

Provisions requiring employers to prove that they cannot find a suitable American applicant before bringing in a foreign worker should remain in place – we have to protect our people first. But we also have to be mindful of the reality, as a Republican former Governor has said, that for many employers "the actual alternative to importing workers is not hiring more Americans but exporting jobs."[220]

People may find this counterintuitive, but the data shows that importing skilled workers *does* create American jobs. According to a recent study, for every 100 foreign-born graduates of a U.S. master's or Ph.D. program who stay in America working in a STEM field, over 250 jobs are created for America workers.[221] In addition to creating jobs, these workers make their fair share of contributions to our tax base. Data from 2009 show that the average foreign-born adult with an advanced degree paid almost $23,000 in federal, state, and Social Security and Medicare taxes, while their families received benefits just 10 percent that size.[222] More jobs and less debt – bringing in more brains is a no-brainer.

The greatest priority is ensuring that we retain the foreign-born STEM students who are already here studying at our universities. In my home state of Pennsylvania, we have well over 200 colleges and universities, many of which have nationally ranked STEM programs. And when I meet foreign-born students in these fields, I think of what Governor Mitt Romney said during the Iowa Presidential Straw Poll in 2011: "If someone comes here and gets a PhD in physics, that's the person I'd like to staple a green card to their diploma, rather than saying to them to go home." Not only should we staple a green card to their diploma, we should give them a shorter path to full citizenship as a further incentive to use their American education in the American economy. And because so much STEM growth is occurring in the green manufacturing sector, green cards can mean more green jobs for the rest of our economy.

If we're serious about businesses big and small having access to innovators, if we're serious about the rebirth of "Made in America" manufacturing, and if we're serious about renewing our national investments, such as in infrastructure, then we must hold on to these STEM graduates who exemplify the American ethic. Not only will they bring new knowledge to our economy, but they will create jobs for American workers and increase our tax base. This isn't about opening the floodgates – it's about using government to empower the needed rugged individuals of the world to continue to come to this country and contribute to our common economic enterprise.

Reducing Recidivism to Increase Productivity

Each year, I spend Veterans' Day and/or Armed Forces Day at a Pennsylvania prison. I do so because I believe many of the veterans who served our country and ended up incarcerated are behind bars because we failed them after they left the military. Last year, I visited my fellow veterans at Graterford Penitentiary for the 25th anniversary of the prison's Vietnam Veterans Chapter. Not all the veterans at Graterford are from Vietnam – too many are there from the more recent wars in Afghanistan and Iraq.

As I walked down the center corridor of the prison among the inmates, I could only imagine how tough the walks were for these men when they went "outside the wire" in a foreign land every day for twelve months, not knowing if the loud sound they suddenly heard was a nearby exploding car or a suicide bomber bent on their destruction. Or how it felt when your next step might set off a buried booby-trap, taking off a part of you, or apart all of you. These men went back to do it again the next year, and then the next, over and over again, with every footstep, on every day. I watched with deep respect as each of the incarcerated veterans was called up by name as other inmates softly hummed the Battle Hymn of the Republic. As the last prisoner strode up and turned, pride on his sorrowful face, the silent prison population rose as one to clap thunderously in appreciation for these veterans' service.

The men with whom I visited were paying for the consequences of the untreated scars that they received while serving our country. During Vietnam, this nation had not heard of Post-Traumatic Stress Disorder (PTSD), let alone known how to treat it. It is no wonder that many veterans from that war became addicted to some drug that eases painful memories – that, unfortunately, was their safe harbor when our country failed to provide one. Even today, too many of the veterans of our two most recent wars are relying on devastating substances that have eased their pain but ruined their lives. These veterans ended up in prison because their service led to PTSD, their PTSD led to drug or alcohol addiction, and their addiction led to joblessness, homelessness, and crime. And because of their criminal convictions, they also had their veteran benefits discontinued.

As a nation, we should be very concerned about the welfare of our veterans. They have served our country honorably, but some of them have ended up on the wrong side of the law because we have failed to provide them with the necessary medical and emotional support once they have come home. Worse still, once they have entered our correction systems, we have failed to provide the proper correction and treatment. Most of them will eventually finish their sentences and rejoin society – what have we done to prepare them to integrate into our workforce and contribute to the American economy? And, beyond our veterans, what about *the rest* of the prison population who are, too often, trapped in a cycle of recidivism?

Today, the United States locks up 2.4 million people in our prisons or jails.[223] We have the highest incarceration rate in the world – greater than both China and Russia.[224] Compounding the problem is the fact that about half of these prisoners will end up back in jail after they are released.[225] With so many prisoners to house, it is no surprise that one in nine state government employees work in corrections.[226] And while the cost of housing a prisoner can amount to tens of thousands of dollars a year, it also counts against the tax dollars we could be earning from a prisoner's gainful employment. This is an immense problem, but if we can reduce recidivism and successfully reintegrate people into our workforce, it's an immense opportunity.

I joined the Navy during the Vietnam War era when judges seemed to still be saying to young truants and offenders, "It's prison or the Navy." Many a young man back then was given an opportunity for "re-entry" to civilian life through either a two or four – or even a twenty – year hitch in our service. They were good kids; they just needed a chance and a helping hand. We gave them remedial education – even a GED – along with a skill for a job. We were authoritative as needed, but also gave them career and life counseling, from their life skills to their family challenges, including housing. We ensured their physical and mental health, and had drug and alcohol rehab (that is, until 1979, when it became only alcohol, as drug usage became a dismissible offense). And boy did they perform.

My experience has taught me that successful re-entry means a great deal for our nation. In the Navy, we provided programs that met the needs of our sailors because we needed them to be able to contribute to our common mission. President George W. Bush had it right when he launched a $300 million re-entry initiative, saying that "America is the land of the second chances, and when the gates of the prison open, the path ahead should lead to a better life." We are a nation of rugged individuals each seeking to make a better life, but one even better when all are capable of contributing fully to our common enterprise of prosperity.

Unfortunately, President Bush's initiative failed because too much of its money was put into programs that failed to use evidence-based metrics including accountable benchmarks and measurable results. Everybody wants to reduce recidivism, but our programs must be based on what works. So far, our government – and broader society on the whole – has been getting it wrong.

In 2001, a review of 10,000 reentry programs over 25 years could find only 19 that underwent evaluations for effectiveness, and only nine of those used a methodology that came close to professional standards.[227] The recent years-long evaluation of the "Serious and Violent Offender Reentry Program" involving 69 agencies and millions of dollars concluded that there were little, if any, positive outcomes for reentry from all this effort.[228] The National Reentry Resource Center clearinghouse, which is intended to provide guidance on evidence-based reentry programs, so far provides only a few dozen examples of programs with metrics to analyze effectiveness. And while few studies professionally evaluate *recidivism*, even fewer measure other equally-significant criteria such as work, wages, and social involvement that can give us a measure of the impact of a program in terms of *reintegration*. The record remains poor and anecdotal.

Fortunately, however, we do have a thin diet of rigorously evaluated reentry programs in order to challenge decision makers to think more substantively about effective solutions. RAND Corporation recently concluded a comprehensive study of 30 years worth of data on correctional education for the incarcerated to determine which programs are most effective. The analysis found that inmates who participated in correctional education programs (GED, vocational, and post-secondary) had 43 percent lower odds of recidivating within three years than inmates who did not participate.[229] As a result, almost $1 million in re-incarceration costs are saved for every $170,000 invested in education programs.[230] Additionally, the study found that inmates who participated had a 13 percent higher chance of employment than those who didn't participate.[231] Unfortunately, as comprehensive as the study was, it concluded that the current literature did not provide an answer as to *what* program elements are associated with effective programs.[232]

One recent effort that is showing promising results is a pilot program in Iowa that provides released inmates with mental illness an extra 60 days of medication in addition to the standard 30 days. Patients with chronic mental illness who received the extra 60 days of medication had a 3 percent likelihood of having ended up back in prison over the course of the 90 day period, compared with 11 percent of patients who did not receive the additional medication.[233] The program has only existed for two years, but if it continues to prove successful, then it can serve as a model for other states; it would also be just the kind of program that federal block grants could support.

These results should be instructive to our leaders. Start to end, those who manage programs aimed at reducing recidivism and those who research them must be teamed up to operate side-by-side to evaluate and create programs that work. A task force should no longer be judged by its recommended policy, but by the success of it. Continuing to throw money at ineffective programs will waste not only our fiscal investment, but worse, the human capital that our nation needs – a person "that works" because the program does. The allocation of taxpayer dollars should therefore be the direct result of adherence to both program accountability and outcome measurement.

Americans want to give a second chance to those in our nation's jails and prisons who are willing to contribute to our common enterprise – but we need accountable leaders who will ensure we're making an investment that truly pays dividends.

In the previous chapters I have mentioned the ways in which we are an exceptional nation – that despite the challenges we have made great achievements for ourselves and the world. We have every right to be proud. At the same time, we as Americans must also realize that the United States is very much an unfinished nation, and that it is the responsibility of every citizen, every institution, and every generation to keep writing our collective history and perfecting our society. This is a monumental task, especially for a continental democracy as vast as ours, competing in an increasingly globalized economy and complicated world.

As such, we need all hands on deck to help us chart our better history in the future and win in this competitive world. We need to create opportunities for all Americans, armed with their own individual strengths, to contribute in their own individual ways. A good place for us to start is to be faithful to what we have always tried to be as a nation: that we are a land of new chances and second chances – for those who want to come here to start anew and for those who want to find a better path forward after having stumbled in life. America has enough room for those who want to do better and, by doing so, contribute to our common enterprise.

Section IV
Restoring Our Promises – I've Got Your Six

(*"I've got your six"* is a term we use in the military to mean *"I've got your back"* – your *"six o'clock"* position.)

Chapter 9

Serving Those Who Served

W hen General George Washington established the first military award in our new American Army – a piece of purple cloth, which was the forerunner of today's Purple Heart – he directed that it would be awarded only to enlisted men and not to officers. General Washington did so because he wanted to highlight the idea that in our new military – and in our new American society – leadership in service of our nation could come from every individual, and each and every one could rise to the top. The example set by Washington has remained constant throughout the history of our armed services – and our nation. Since our nation's founding, America's rugged individuals, regardless of rank or birth, have been standing up to fight for our common enterprise, holding themselves personally accountable for protecting our shared purpose.

And yet, too often, our leaders in Washington have failed to honor the work that these veterans have done for our nation and the sacrifices that they have made. When I think of their sacrifices, I am reminded of a painting I used to pass regularly in the Pentagon. The picture hangs across from the Secretary of Defense's office and depicts a young couple kneeling in a house of worship – a servicemember next to his wife, with their young child beside them. Under the painting is an inscription from the Book of Isaiah: "Whom shall I send? And who will go for us?" And Isaiah replied, "Here am I. Send me."

During my 31 years in the Navy, I always wondered why so many young men and women said, "Here am I, send me." In the Revolutionary War, historians wrote about bloody footprints in the snow the night of the Delaware River crossing; in the Civil War, soldiers walked alongside one another as grapeshot was fired upon them; in World War I and II immigrants like my father took up arms to defend their adopted nation; tunnel rats in Vietnam dove down dark, narrow passages; and, the men and women in the wars in Afghanistan and Iraq went "outside the wire" every day of their tours.

Why do they do it? I've never determined the exact explanation. But the closest I've come to finding an answer happened at a dinner one evening that President Clinton held in the White House. The President was about to go to Normandy to speak at the 50th anniversary of the "D-Day" invasion, and he had asked five veterans of the Normandy landing to dine with him. He also invited a group of historians who had written about the battle where the world's greatest generation turned the tides of history.

During the dinner, one of the historians told the President that, during the landing on the sands of Normandy, almost all of the officers were killed immediately, because in the Germans' Teutonic mind, if you cut off the head (the officer corps) then the body (the enlisted corps) would collapse. Little did the Germans understand the American army, he said. Here were these young men, many only teenagers, clawing their way up the wet sands of Omaha Beach trying to hide from the hell of the shells coming down on them from the white bluffs above, leaderless, looking at one another and then simply saying "we're going to get the hell off this beach." In twos, threes, and fours, they took those bluffs and over the next year they went on to defeat Germany.

The historian then looked at President Clinton and said "Mr. President, don't ever forget that whatever 'it' is, that 'it' that we somehow instill in the youth of America to be like that, Mr. President – *that* is the national treasure you must most cherish."

This historian's story of those brave young soldiers reminded me of the motto we had on the very first ship I commanded, the USS Samuel B. Roberts, the third ship named for a soldier killed in the Battle of Guadalcanal in 1942. The first "Sammy B" ship had fought in the Pacific during World War II at the Battle of Leyte Gulf. Nearby was a ship upon which my father was serving. As the first Sammy B was sinking, the Captain gave the order to abandon ship and sent the Executive Officer to quickly scour the ship and make sure everyone was safely off. At the aft gun mount, the XO found Gunner's Mate Third Class Paul H. Carr.

Everyone knows someone like Gunner Carr – just a good guy. Senior and junior officers and enlisted alike loved being around him. On this day, Gunner Carr's gun mount had been destroyed, one of his legs had been almost torn off, and he was cradling a round in his arms as he tried to get up with his one good leg and load the shell into the breach to keep fighting. The XO took the shell out of Gunner Carr's arms, laid it on the deck and left to get help. When he returned with the other men, they found that Gunner Carr had crawled over, picked up that shell, and was again trying to get up on his one leg and keep fighting. They again took the shell out of his arms, and they placed him on a stretcher and took him to a life boat where Gunner Carr soon died.

In writing the battle report on the loss of the ship, the ship's Captain wrote the words that later became our motto on another Sammy B a half-century later: that there was "No Higher Honor" than to have served with a man such as Gunner Carr during the war.

During my command of an aircraft carrier battle group in Afghanistan, I saw firsthand an example of that willingness to sacrifice oneself for the common purpose. Shortly after arriving in the Northern Indian Ocean for retaliatory strikes against al-Qaeda and the Taliban, I sent eight pilots on a mission. That group included seven guys who had served in the first Gulf War, but with them went someone we in the Navy call a "nugget" – an aviator who had not been overseas and over a foreign country before, and certainly not in combat. She was 27 years old, a brand new F-18 pilot. On that mission, she became the one who disregarded the standing order not to dive below 20,000 feet unless first requesting permission, so that commanders had time (through other means) to see if the Taliban might have shoulder-fired Stinger missiles down below.

That night, there were U.S. Special Forces on the ground below, and four had died in an enemy ambush. The four remaining warriors radioed to the aircraft above that there was no time to wait because the enemy was both closing rapidly and was already too close for laser-guided munitions. They had only moments left, and needed someone to strafe so that they could get out of there in the confusion. The 27-year-old "nugget," alone that night as the closest pilot to the chaos, didn't hesitate to ask for permission and, putting herself in danger of being shot down, strafed three times in the middle of the night from 20,000 feet to 3,000 feet. Because of what she did, the Special Forces were able to carry their dead comrades and make it home alive.

In this case, that pilot rightfully disregarded standing orders at great risk to herself and at a minimum, to her career because in her judgment, greater mission – and the special bond we have in the armed services – overruled her own individual risks. That special bond comes both from a warrior's refusal to let their fellow service member down as well as a complete willingness to give their life for that of their comrade in the same common cause.

But sadly, when these men and women return from combat, our leaders have often failed at providing our veterans with the care and transitional support that they need. Too often, politicians pay tribute to veterans only with words and public fanfare – not through action. With yet another generation of warriors coming home from the Global War on Terror, we must resolve to restore our solemn promise that those who serve our nation will themselves always be served.

Bridging the Gap from Boots to Business

To begin, it is nothing short of a moral outrage that so many of our lawmakers were willing to spend trillions[234] on the wars in Iraq and Afghanistan but unwilling to spend a few billion on jobs programs for returning veterans. When you make a decision to send troops abroad, you have to calculate the cost of transitioning them back home. The failure to do so is a dereliction of congressional duty. But aside from the moral imperative of keeping our solemn promise to support the troops, increasing the opportunities for returning veterans is also about taking full advantage of their human capital for our shared economic benefit.

These rugged individuals who were willing to say "Here am I" are highly trained, self-motivated, and bring a can-do attitude to the workplace. Yet, the unemployment rate for veterans of the Iraq and Afghanistan wars hit 9 percent in mid-2014, while the national unemployment rate was a full 3 percent lower.[235] The reasons behind this are concerning – surely related to post-traumatic stress disorder, traumatic brain injury, and other hidden battlefield wounds (more on this later). But we must do everything in our power to let our veterans know that when they return home looking to rejoin the workforce, we are willing to say "I've got your six."

As I said in a previous chapter, a first step is expanding entrepreneurial opportunities for veterans who want to start a small business through increased access to business loans. Because veterans are trained to take initiative and solve problems, it is no surprise that nearly one in 10 small businesses are owned by veterans. In fact, veterans are 45 percent more likely to be self-employed than the rest of the population.[236] If government can play a more robust role as a facilitator for veterans to start their own small businesses, more are likely to do so, creating new jobs along the way for the rest of our economy.

Similarly, we must give every employer a greater incentive to hire those who have served our nation. The VOW to Hire Heroes Act was a good start, giving a tax credit of up to $5,600 for hiring veterans who have been looking for a job for six months and $9,600 for businesses who hire former warriors with disabilities.[237] This is a good start, but I believe we must do better for our veterans. That said, no veteran wants to be included in a veterans-focused program without the commensurate skills; and such programs partly address the debt we owe those who sacrificed for us by ensuring veterans a fair opportunity as they reenter the workforce.

In view of the above, I would support immediately raising the $5,600 and $9,600 limits to $10,000 and $15,000, respectively, and I would make any decrease on that cap contingent upon a drop in the unemployment rate for veterans. Our tax credits should incentivize American employment, not corporate largesse.

As we assess the effectiveness of how we help our veterans, we should look at programs that have been proven to work across the states. For example, the Texas Veterans Leadership Program has shown particular promise as a national grassroots model.[238] This Texas program is managed by a team of 23 Iraq and Afghanistan veterans who keep track of every military discharge paper and unemployment claim filed by a veteran. Then, team members directly contact each veteran and offer to serve as a link between those veterans and businesses looking to hire.[239] In a single month, the centers in Texas' Brazos Valley assisted almost 400 veterans in finding employment.[240]

Likewise, California's Employment Development Department has been operating a Veterans Academy program with a track record of success.[241] The Academy consists of 10 classes over a five week period that train veterans how to use job search technology, assesses military skills transferrable to the workplace, and provides training on résumés, cover letters, and the job interview process. At the end of the program, veterans receive a Work Opportunity Tax Credit form and are referred to employers who earn the tax credit by hiring the veteran. As a result, about 90 percent of those who graduate from the Veterans Academy find employment.

If the federal government is going to be investing in bringing veterans into the workforce, we cannot afford to just throw money at the problem. Just like the retraining programs I mentioned in the previous chapters, we should be investing our money in proven programs for veterans that have already succeeded in various parts of the country. We want our rugged returning veterans to be all they can be, but we have to do it with full accountability so that we can all benefit from the shared investment.

A Helping Hand for Our Homeless Heroes

The number of homeless veterans speaks volumes about our failure to confront and heal the burdens our warriors have carried home from war. That's why when I got to Congress, I voted to expand housing assistance for homeless veterans by providing at least 20,000 rental vouchers a year and creating a new supportive housing program for our former warriors at the Department of Housing and Urban Development (HUD). I also introduced legislation to make it more affordable for homeless veterans to receive housing assistance through the program. The HUD-VASH voucher program has served over 70,000 veterans since 2008,[242] and the number of homeless veterans has fallen by a third since 2010 – from 75,000 to under 50,000 on any given night.[243] But we still have a long way to go.

I am proud of the gains made by the federal programs I fought to fund, but I have also been impressed by the successful efforts made by individual cities in achieving measurable benchmarks toward ending veteran homelessness. The hardest-to-reach group of homeless veterans is those who have been "chronically" homeless, meaning that they have been homeless for at least a year or repeatedly homeless over the span of many years. In this category, two cities – Phoenix and Salt Lake City – have instituted programs with proven results.

After a three-year effort, Phoenix became the first city in the country to end chronic veteran homelessness. Phoenix used a "housing first" strategy, meaning that homeless veterans and their families were given housing *before* being required to prove sobriety or pass a drug test.[244] In the past, the promise of housing was used as a "carrot" to reward veterans with drug and alcohol problems, with the "stick" being continued homelessness. The housing first strategy recognizes instead that someone is more likely to be able to kick an addiction if they first have a safe and stable place to stay.[245] Then, once housed, veterans were assigned a caseworker and provided with health services and even job training.[246]

Phoenix's program succeeded not only because of the new philosophy, but because of the integration of multiple groups both inside and outside of government, including the Phoenix Housing and Human Services Department, the Arizona Coalition to End Homelessness, and the VA National Homeless Veterans Outreach Campaign, among others. As a result, Phoenix went from 222 chronically homeless veterans in 2010 to zero by the end of 2013.[247]

In part due to such successes, at the beginning of 2014, Salt Lake City soon followed Phoenix in housing all of its chronically homeless vets.[248] Again, the program was successful because it was a joint enterprise among multiple levels of government and private sector partners. To get private actors involved, Salt Lake City's mayor announced a "Housing Veterans Month." He didn't do it just to get a good headline; he did it to encourage landlords across the city to offer their extra units, which led to 40 property owners coming forward and partnering with the city's public housing authority.[249] At about the same time, private organizations partnered with the Department of Veterans Affairs (VA) so that VA staff would operate at homeless shelters instead of just the VA hospital, putting them in direct contact with chronically homeless vets. Shortly thereafter, the roughly 100 chronically homeless vets identified by local shelters and other nonprofits in Salt Lake City had all been housed.

We owe it to our homeless heroes to replicate these successful programs across the country in similar cities. It is not enough for the federal government to simply spend money – we have to spend it on programs that work and that leverage other assets and offer measurable benchmarks for accountability. We owe that to our veterans and to ourselves as taxpayers.

Revamping the VA

As a Congressman, I met with VA officials over troubling reports of unsanitary VA nursing homes in Pennsylvania, including one patient with an open foot wound left unattended so long that maggots were found falling from the lesion. One VA Medical Center broke federal law by drawing blood samples from veterans for a research project without their consent, and also underwent a scathing investigation to determine how nearly 100 prostate cancer patients were treated with excessively high or low levels of brachytherapy radiation due to a lack of oversight – and no one had been held accountable.

As a veteran, I share the concerns of those who question inexcusable practices at VA hospitals, some brought to light in recent scandals. But at the same time, I recognize there has been a vast improvement at VA facilities compared to when I entered service in the Vietnam era. As a young sailor home on leave in Delaware County, Pennsylvania, in the mid-1980s, I suddenly had excruciating stomach pains and was directed to Philadelphia's VA hospital. I didn't want to go because of the VA's poor reputation when I had entered service over a decade earlier, but thankfully things had improved there: I underwent a skillful emergency appendectomy and follow-up treatment. The key today is to fix what's wrong, and recognize that there is much that's right to keep.

For example, during my time in Congress – working under that Navy rubric, "expect what you inspect" – I authored the Transparency Act mandating that all VA inspection reports be made public upon completion. In the cases of maggots in wounds and improper radiation treatment, there wouldn't have been corrective actions if it weren't for a Freedom of Information Act (FOIA) request that finally made the results public.

I also worked with the VA's neurologists to move forward on providing veterans the option of having post-traumatic stress disorder (PTSD) and traumatic brain injury treatments handled – with VA oversight –

in a veteran's community-based private health center, so that veterans could be treated within their community of support. We also need to change the VA policy of not transferring the medical records of incarcerated veterans to prisons because without a full and transparent sharing of crucial medical data between health care professionals, we run a higher risk of making wrong diagnoses and providing subpar care. And while we were successful in re-enrolling thousands of "Priority 8" veterans making as little as $30,000 who were locked out of VA services by a congressional vote in 2003, we still don't have all of them back in.

I am immensely frustrated by those in Congress who excoriate the VA but were the very ones who repeatedly voted against budgets that would have addressed much of the VA's problems. Unquestionably, those VA personnel responsible for the recent scandal must be held accountable. And we need to mandate transparency measures so we can hold those responsible to benchmarks that make the VA more responsive to veterans. But we also must appreciate the high level of performance in much of the VA, including so many employees who care deeply about the well-being of those who have served to protect our nation.

Let's not overlook the fact that, for an institution that currently serves about eight million veterans, the VA has plenty of bright spots. A recent study found that the risk of death was lower for a veteran if he or she is treated in a VA hospital than in a civilian hospital under Medicare Advantage. A veteran treated in a VA hospital is 16 percent more likely to receive recommended care than a veteran in a community hospital. The veteran is also 10 percent more likely to receive better care for chronic conditions, and 20 percent more likely to receive better preventative care. In terms of costs, VA care is about 20 percent less expensive than Medicare. And, the VA also has been successful with switching to electronic medical records, which have revolutionized health care for our vets and have been invaluable after natural disasters such as Hurricane Katrina, which destroyed many other hospitals' paper records. Still, like all institutions of its size and scope, the VA can always do better to serve our veterans.

For example, currently our veterans who live in rural areas are particularly underserved. This is a significant problem because about one-third of the veterans served by the VA live in areas considered to be rural or highly rural.[250] Patients who suffer from PTSD, in particular, face the daunting challenge of driving long distances into busy cities, an unnecessary routine that can only serve to exacerbate their condition. In Congress, I co-sponsored the Rural Veterans Health Care Access Act which directed the Secretary of Veterans Affairs to establish and implement a pilot program to provide mental health counseling to eligible veterans at non-VA medical facilities in nearby community health centers.

At present, modern technology offers a high-tech solution that could put care within veterans' reach in the comfort of their own homes. For many veterans today, a potentially promising treatment alternative would be home treatment via digital interface with VA doctors and psychologists, so that they would avoid the stress of travel and stay close to their families. However, as discussed in a previous chapter, rural communities are also plagued by limited wireless/broadband infrastructure. In fact, over half a million veterans enrolled in VA care do not have access to the speeds necessary to teleconnect.[251] Our next infrastructure bill must prioritize the expansion of rural broadband access so that our veterans can take advantage of better connectivity, enhancing their ability to communicate with and receive treatment from their doctors and mental health professionals in faraway cities.

Additionally, we should seek to expand private partnerships between the VA and research universities. In Congress, I met several times with PTSD and traumatic brain injury (TBI) doctors at both the University of Pennsylvania and the VA. I saw firsthand the lessons that can be learned in these public-private partnerships, and I supported legislation to fund new joint initiatives. These investments have proven results: in recent years researchers at the University of Pittsburgh discovered a new way to diagnose TBI through high definition fiber tracking,[252] and at the University of Wisconsin-Madison a new neurostimulation therapy was developed to treat TBI patients.[253] By pulling resources together, the VA and private institutions can collaborate on enhancing technologies and know-how that will be able to save lives and improve the living standards of not just our veterans, but also patients in the civilian realm throughout our country.

***

President Washington wisely noted that "the willingness with which our young people are likely to serve in any war, no matter how justified, shall be directly proportional to how they perceive veterans of earlier wars were treated and appreciated by our nation."

While our leaders are never short of speeches to show this appreciation, their actions too often fall short. When a soldier tells a fellow soldier "I've got your six," their performance backs up the promise. We must now renew our solemn vow of support for those who served – not just with words, but through deeds.

Chapter 10

Standing With Our Seniors

Hubert Humphrey said it well when he noted that the moral test of a government is not only how it treats those who are in the dawn of life, the children; those who are in the shadows of life, the sick, the needy and the handicapped; but also those who are in the twilight of life, the elderly. That's why when I was in Congress, I made it a priority to seek out a meeting with senior citizens almost each and every weekend at senior centers, care facilities, and nursing homes across my district. I did this because I believe strongly that our nation needs their wisdom and experience. At almost every visit, it was hard not to burst with pride at the continued contributions that so many rugged individual seniors, even at advanced ages, were making to our country with the support of the community.

Seniors – a title we will all (hopefully) assume one day – represent our history and memory. They are vital to our families and communities. It is solely from our elders that we can get the invaluable perspective only time and reflection provide. But sadly, many of our seniors are not spending their golden years with a real sense of security. Seniors today are living with an increasing threat of elder abuse, a shortage in the availability of long-term care, and funding problems with Medicare, Medicaid, and Social

Security. And as the 65-plus population grows from 40 million today to more than 70 million in 2030,[254] these problems will only compound if left unaddressed.

Preventing Elder Abuse

Every day, too many of our nation's seniors fall victim to physical, mental, financial, and even sexual abuse. Recent estimates put the annual number of elder abuse victims at four million with the vast majority – almost 90 percent – of cases going unreported.[255] This endemic problem is particularly important in my home state of Pennsylvania, where the more than two million senior citizens in our Commonwealth make up 16 percent of the population.[256] I was taken aback to learn the year I entered Congress that Pennsylvania had seen a 39 percent rise in substantiated reports of elder abuse over the previous year.

And as I met the people behind these statistics at senior groups, I was deeply troubled that we are failing victims including an elderly resident of Pottsville, Pennsylvania who had $84,000 drained from his bank accounts as he slipped into dementia. He died shortly thereafter. In his old age, this gentleman had become one of the 40 percent of elder abuse victims who faced financial exploitation. Annually, an estimated $3 billion in losses occur as a result of financial abuse of elder victims, with the losses growing each year in tandem with the historic growth in the over-65 segment of the population.[257]

Then there was the elderly Alzheimer's patient who was struck at least six times with a belt buckle by an aide at an assisted living facility in nearby King of Prussia, Pennsylvania. Physical abuse of the elderly leaves more than just bruises; older adults who are abused are three times more likely to die within 10 years than those who are not. A 2004 study cited by the National Center on Elder Abuse estimated the direct medical costs associated with violent injuries to older adults to be over $5.3 billion, which is a cost all of us bear.[258]

My many interactions with seniors informed my legislative agenda during my public life. When I served in Congress, one of my proudest achievements was authoring the Elder Abuse Victims Act, which was the first bill on elder abuse to pass the House of Representatives in 17 years. My bill was an important piece of the broader Elder Justice Act, and it focused mainly on prosecuting those who perpetrate elder abuse. The Elder Abuse Victims Act took significant steps in protecting seniors from abuse by evaluating the effectiveness of state and federal programs, advocacy grants, and prosecution of elder abuse cases.

It also provided for, among other things, funding for elder abuse prosecutorial departments at the local, state, and federal levels; training law enforcement officials on appropriate action in these cases; funding for nurse-investigators who are experts in identifying elder abuse; and, requiring the Attorney General to conduct a study evaluating state programs and practices designed to protect seniors from abuse, neglect, and exploitation.

My bill was aimed at taking tangible steps toward preventing elder abuse across the country, which is why the National Coordinator of the Elder Justice Coalition called the passage of the bill "the most significant vote specifically on elder justice ever taken in the House." Unfortunately, after I left the House of Representatives, Congress failed to appropriate money for my legislation, as well as the broader Elder Justice Act.[259] As a result of this Congressional failure to provide funding, we continue to lack sufficient statistics to analyze elder abuse and suffer from uneven enforcement as a result of a hodgepodge of prosecution across the states. Meanwhile, our seniors continue to experience abuse at startling rates.

I continue to be baffled and appalled at Congress's unwillingness to invest money in elder abuse prevention. When I put forward my $30 million bill, the federal government was spending approximately $153 million on programs addressing elder abuse – which paled in comparison to the $6.7 billion spent on child abuse and the $520 million mandated by the Violence Against Women Act, both measures which I support strongly.[260] Today, the disparity continues. According to a report by the Congressional Research Service, Congress has failed to appropriate discretionary funding for any Elder Justice Act program.[261] And because of this failure of leadership, our seniors continue to fall victim to greater and greater abuses.

Dignity and Self-Determination in Long-Term Care

Of the eight million Americans receiving long-term care, almost 60 percent receive their services at home.[262] This preference for in-home care shouldn't be much of a surprise – all of us want to retain our independence and stay rooted in our own community. And when someone can no longer live completely independently, we don't want them to have to leave their home. At the same time, in-home care is significantly less expensive than care at a facility. Home health aide services have a median national cost of roughly $20 per hour, while the national median daily rate of nursing home care is about $212.[263] So for those who need less than 10 hours of care a day, a per-hour health aid in the familiar comfort of one's own home is very often the preferred choice instead of a nursing home. And because Medicare and Medicaid pay for so much of these services, continuing the shift toward in-home care as opposed to care at a facility saves us all money.

Much of the long-term care provided to seniors isn't necessarily medical; seniors frequently retain their independence through assistance with activities of daily living from home service providers. This includes help with eating, walking, bathing, dressing, transportation, and toileting. While family members can help with much of this, the burden is often too great and outside help is required. The financial and personal preferences for in-home care, however, are tied to availability and affordability of care, both of which our leaders must address.

The issues of availability and affordability are, or course, linked. According to the Paraprofessional Health Institute, the direct-care workforce in 2012 included four million workers, comprising nursing assistants, home health aides, personal care aides,[264] and independent providers employed directly by consumers.[265] Over the next decade alone, we will need to add an estimated 1.6 million workers to that pool.[266] However, many of these jobs tend to be low-paying despite the high-need, largely due to the fact that such jobs are often considered to be low-skill. Even though a consumer may pay $20 to a homecare agency,[267] the national median hourly rate of home health and personal care aides is $10.01 and $9.57, respectively – meaning half of them make less than those rates.[268] As a result of the low wages, many of these workers are themselves reliant on government benefits.

Here's the problem: we are experiencing a high need for workers in a low wage profession; we want our seniors to keep the dignity of living at home safely and at a less expensive rate than a nursing home, while at the same time keeping the cost of care as stable as possible. There isn't a single solution, but by taking a combination of steps, we can gradually move forward toward filling the supply gap and alleviating the financial burden on families.

First, in the short term, it is worth noting that both median hourly wages I listed above are below the minimum wage for which I advocated in a previous chapter. Raising the minimum wage would give in-home workers a step upwards, recognizing the dignity they deserve for caring for our elders with dignity, and reduce the amount of government benefits that we are already providing many of these workers.

Second, just as we need to adjust immediately our formula for STEM visas to compete in the new economy, we will soon have to consider adjusting the formula for work visas for those who care for our seniors retiring from the old economy. Lawmakers will need to make these adjustments based on facts and figures – we should only let homecare workers in when there are not enough homecare workers here already.

Third, we should provide more adequate tax credits and deductions for family members who provide care for their elders. For example, one of the imperfections of the Affordable Care Act is that it only allows a deduction for medical expenses that exceed 10 percent of income. Prior to the ACA, deductions were permitted for medical expenses that exceeded 7.5 percent of income. We must bring this level back down to 7.5 immediately and, as our national debt gets under control, seek to reduce it as low as 5 percent. Similarly, the dependency deduction requires that you are paying more than 50 percent of a parent's support costs. This should be lowered to 25 percent. By easing the financial burden on families who are already working, essentially, a part-time job as caregiver, we incentivize less expensive and more personal care while at the same time decreasing the burden on Medicare, Medicaid, and the in-home care market.

Fourth, given the fact that Alzheimer's disease almost always leads to long-term services and support and that one in eight Americans over 65 has Alzheimer's,[269] we must do more to cure this terrible disease. In Pennsylvania alone, more than half a million people suffer from Alzheimer's and there are close to 450,000 family caregivers.[270] Not only would a cure save families the pain and hardship of seeing one of their elders fall victim to the disease, but the money invested in finding a cure would generate untold dividends in decreasing the cost of elder care – not to mention a reduction in financial abuse of elders. We should be increasing funding for the National Institutes of Health's cutting-edge research and clinical trials on Alzheimer's – not cutting it as too many shortsighted lawmakers have voted to do.

Ferreting Out Fraud in Medicare

Although the Affordable Care Act has added 13 years to the life of the Medicare trust fund through cost-savings and a slowdown in the growth rate of premiums, the government has yet to rein in the exorbitant costs of Medicare fraud. According to the GAO, Medicare financed health care services for 51 million people at a cost of $604 billion in 2013.[271] However, according to law enforcement officials, as much as 10 percent of Medicare spending constitutes fraudulent claims – as much as $60 billion dollars in 2013 – and only $4.3 billion in fraudulent funds were recovered.[272] This 7 percent recovery rate is unacceptably low. Fortunately, though, we are beginning to make progress using smart technology to track down the fraudsters and prevent overpayments.

According to an investigative report by the *Wall Street Journal*, the Centers for Medicare and Medicaid Services' three-year-old Fraud Prevention System is showing impressive results in using predictive technology to identify providers who might be defrauding the system. The Fraud Prevention System directly resulted in close to 500 investigations in 2013, preventing over $210 million improper fee-for-service payments, which is double the amount from the program's first year.[273] Similarly, the *Wall Street Journal* also found that since the Medicare Fraud Strike Force added seven additional offices across the country, they have already charged 350 providers with fraud compared to 122 when the strike force only had two offices.[274]

These initiatives, among other healthcare fraud and abuse program, are an excellent investment for taxpayers. With an estimated return on investment of $7.90 for each $1.00 spent, we should expand funding for such successful programs.[275] But unfortunately, because of sequestration, many of the successful fraud prevention initiatives we have developed through new technology over the last few years are seeing massive budget cuts coupled with an expiration of supplemental funding.[276] We must exempt from future sequestration and other budget reductions all fraud-prevention programs that are proven to save taxpayer dollars. I believe we can achieve bipartisan agreement that it is worth spending one taxpayer dollar to save eight taxpayer dollars, especially when it means that our seniors will reap the benefits of a more solvent Medicare.

One last item worth noting on Medicare fraud is that much of this fee-for-service fraud results from our current "quantity of care" model – something that the Affordable Care Act aims to transition us away from and, instead, move toward a model based more on the "quality of care." Under the Accountable Care Organization model, which I discussed in great length in a previous chapter, physicians are no longer paid for the amount of services they provide, thereby removing the perverse incentive to commit the particular type of fraud that has been so prevalent in the fee-for-service model. This is yet another reason why I have been, and continue to be, a strong proponent of the ACA.

Reversing the Regressive Nature of the Social Security Tax

If we're serious about strengthening the Social Security system that our seniors so greatly rely on for their daily needs, then it's time we have a serious discussion about ensuring its long-term solvency. The reality of the situation is that there is not one solution to fix Social Security, but rather a myriad of measures that have to be taken with pieces drawn from a variety of fact-based proposals.

One piece that too many of our leaders avoid discussing is the cap on the top end of the payroll tax, which is sometimes called the "tax max." This is so little discussed by elected officials that many people are not aware the current payroll tax limit on earnings is capped at $117,000.[277] What this means is that workers who make up to $117,000 in a year pay the Social Security tax on every dollar earned – however, if you make for example $1,000,000 this year then you only have to pay the Social Security tax on the first $117,000.

Put another way, someone who makes a million dollars a year only pays the Social Security tax on every 10 cents he earns while the vast majority of Americans pay tax on every single dollar they earn. A millionaire gets a reduced-price for their lunch; a middle class worker pays the full-ticket.

But that's not the worst of it. Let's look at some historic data covering this high-end "tax max" over the last 30 or so years. In 1983, President Reagan and congressional Democrats made their "great compromise" to design the tax max to cover 90 percent of all wage and salary income. And at that time, the funding formula did cover 90 percent of taxable wages, and about 6 percent of covered workers earned above the tax-max in 1983.[278] Fast-forward to 2006, the year before the great recession: only 83.6 percent of taxable wages were covered but still about 6 percent of covered workers earned above the tax max.[279]

What this means is that even though the same percentage of the population is making above the tax max today as 1983, wealth has become so concentrated that the top few are getting an even better bargain than the top got in the heyday of trickle-down economics.

The Social Security Board of Trustees estimated in their 2014 report that the retirement program is expected to cover benefits until 2033.[280] Seeing that date approaching, many of our leaders suggest we should solve the insolvency by privatizing Social Security or slashing cost of living adjustments. What we *should* be doing is looking at pieces of the puzzle – like the $117,000 cap – and figure out how we can adjust the formula to extend the promise of Social Security to future generations.

What I'm proposing is not a case of taking away from the rich to give to the poor. It's about making sure we are all contributing a fair share for the benefits we all receive. Bringing fairness to the payroll tax is long overdue – especially when you consider that under our overall U.S. tax policy, the top fifth of the population receives 66 percent of tax benefits.[281] It's no surprise that a Republican Senator recently said that "[t]he government's social safety net, which has long existed to catch those who are down and help them get back up, is now being used as a hammock by some millionaires, some who are paying less taxes than average middle class families."[282] Fairness should not be considered a radical agenda, and our leaders must work harder toward restoring the promise of retirement security for hardworking Americans. We want our highest earners to succeed as rugged individuals, but caring for our common heritage – our seniors – is a shared responsibility we all must join in upholding.

We are a nation that prides itself on our endless energy, youthful optimism, and rugged individualism. We embrace the language of innovation, entrepreneurialism, and the draw of constant change – a belief that we should always focus not on the past, but on the future. This is admirable, and it is what helps make our nation great.

But embedded within this drive for continuous renewal must be a healthy respect for the previous generations, those who have put in the hard work to make their tomorrow, our present, better than before. The young entrepreneurs and dedicated workers of yesteryear are our seniors today, and they have made just as much contribution to our nation as the innovative thinkers and rugged individuals of younger generations.

What will define our character as a nation – our ship of state – is not only how fast we move through the rough but expansive sea of history, but our commitment to all the hands on deck who have served yesterday, today, and tomorrow. We must be a society that takes care of our own, whether we are in the dawn, shadows, or twilight of our lives – saying "I've got your six." Fairness and kindness, after all, know no bounds or generations.

Section V

RESTORING OUR FUTURE – FULL SPEED AHEAD

Chapter 11

Investing in Education Pays the Best Interest for Our National Interest

Maybe it's because I'm the son of a teacher, but I truly don't believe we can overinvest in knowledge. Benjamin Franklin was absolutely right when he said that "an investment in knowledge always pays the best interest." That's because in America, our common prosperity is built by rugged individuals who need nothing more than the tools to succeed – education being the most powerful. As a military man, I have always viewed education as our "homeland defense" because our nation's ability to adapt to ever-changing security threats depends on a skilled workforce that can out-innovate our competitors in the 21st century economic and national security environment. As a father, I view our youth as our "national treasure" because it is our children who will continue to make our country prosper for generations to come, keeping the American Dream alive.

Among the first public schools in America was one founded in 1684 in Philadelphia, not far from where I grew up. By order of the governor of Pennsylvania, the school was to serve "all children and servants, male and female," charging "the rich at reasonable rates, and the poor to be maintained and schooled for nothing."[283] The provincial council approved the creation of the school for all because Pennsylvania needed *everybody* to contribute to our shared common wealth.

This realization is what made Pennsylvania – and the rest of the country – so exceptional. We focused our collective enterprise on waterways, roadways, mass communication, energy infrastructure, and public schools, and we mandated that every child go to public school so that at the end of 12 years these rugged individuals would contribute to our shared growth and find novel uses for those roadways and waterways.

But today, our education system is failing to prepare our "national treasure" to contribute to our "homeland defense." Internationally, our students are falling behind other developed countries in math, science, and reading.[284] Here at home, student success too often depends not only on the state in which a child is born, but whether she lives in the city or on the farm. And for the eight in 10 who manage to graduate from high school,[285] their options are limited by higher education costs that have grown faster than inflation, health care, and housing.[286]

Now more than ever, business leaders in the private sector are making the connection between corporate needs and educated human capital. The 150-member group of CEOs on the Committee Encouraging Corporate Philanthropy recently released data showing that K-12 and higher education received the greatest share of all corporate giving in 2012, reflecting the business need for the best possible "future workforce talent pool."[287] We need leaders in government who understand – like our business leaders do – that investing in education is not just for the benefit of students but for our entire nation.

Improving Performance and Maintaining Competitiveness, through Accountability

My experience in the Navy taught me that the best decisions are made based on facts and data, and that once a decision is made you need to have benchmarks and measurements in place to determine the effectiveness of a course of action. I believe that, to a large extent, our national inability to make meaningful policy about K-12 education is the result of the lack of assessable data on what students are expected to know in each grade, combined with each state using measurement systems intended to artificially inflate their own numbers.

A report by the *Wall Street Journal* analyzing data from New York recently provided an example of this problem. In 2009, 86 percent of the students who took New York's standardized tests had "proficient or better" scores in math.[288] These results were roundly criticized across the state as being artificially inflated, so New York raised the cutoffs for "proficient" the following year. Accordingly, 61 percent of students ranked "proficient" in math. Then, in 2013, when New York became one of the first states to use new tests aligned to national Common Core standards, less than one third of students were found to have shown "proficiency" in math.

What this means is that policymakers have been stuck using data without definition. As a result, instead of making decisions about how to increase educational attainment, states are simply deciding to redefine their terms. Yes, the *tests* may be *standardized*, but they haven't been linked to any actual *standard*. Teachers can't measure their methods, parents don't know if their child is falling behind, and students spend sweat and tears taking tests that don't improve their skills.

All hope, however, is not lost.

The final set of data from the New York example, I believe, has great promise. When 45 states and the District of Columbia adopted the National Governors Association's Common Core State Standards, they did so in part to reform the toxic testing that resulted from the way No Child Left Behind (NCLB) was implemented. The high-stakes testing regime implemented under NCLB focused on filling in bubbles on multiple choice exams to assess whether students were "proficient" in state standards. Each state had to demonstrate that they were making adequate yearly progress toward closing an achievement gap between students, based on their own state standards. Reacting to this model, it is no surprise that standards were set just low enough for the poorest-performing students to attain a state's lowest achievement level.

Military trained, my perspective is that because we recruit from all 50 states, we have to know what numbers mean. Our national security is hindered when someone graduates high school from, say, Mississippi with low standards but their "scores" are "equal" to Pennsylvania's – just as our economic security is hindered when colleges recruit from all 50 states and don't know whether "proficient" means "proficient."

With the Common Core, however, a national standard is set by describing what each student in each grade level in each state should know in English language arts/literacy and mathematics to prepare students for a job or college. The standards are benchmarks, not curricula. A school's curriculum will remain locally developed. There is no required reading list except for the Declaration of Independence, the preamble to the Constitution, the Bill of Rights, and Lincoln's Second Inaugural Address.[289] The standards say where each student should be, not how to get there. They were developed by teachers, school administrators, education experts, and parents.[290]

Once the standards are adopted, modern testing focusing on problem-solving instead of bubble-filling will be put in place, creating accountability to a common standard across the country – that our businesses and colleges can rely upon. This, in turn, will produce data that is actually usable because even if states still try to play the "proficient" definition game, we will have the national context to know whether their metric is mislaid or meaningless.

Based on my conversations with educators and parents, the Common Core standards are not perfectly written – especially in the lower grade levels. I have read many of the distressingly obtuse questions written for Common Core Practice Tests, and we absolutely have to do better.[291] But the idea of a common standard is crucial if we are serious about getting reliable data on whether our students have the skills necessary to transition into higher education or enter the workforce by graduation. Good decisions require good data, and assessing progress requires meaningful benchmarks.

I am also encouraged by the conversations I have had with educators about a new generation of computer-based tests that teachers and students can use to identify gaps in learning in real-time – instead of in retrospect at the end of the year when it's too late. Using an adaptive algorithm, students are presented with questions that get harder or easier based on the answers the student gives.

If my daughter is getting all the easy and intermediate questions correct, she is presented with harder questions to gauge where her learning has progressed. If she gets a few questions wrong, the algorithm adapts to revert back to the intermediate level so she won't get discouraged and so that her actual skill level can be measured.[292]

The results of the test would then be submitted in real-time to my daughter's teacher, who can immediately identify where she (and the rest of the class) needs help individually. That way, when the big tests come at the end of the year, my daughter and her teacher have greater confidence in meeting the benchmarks aligned with the Common Core. This is what we want our tests to do – provide guidance for learning instead of penalties in funding. Are the algorithms perfect? No. Should they be used to measure essay writing? No. Do they completely replace a teacher's intuition for when his or her students "get it?" No. But by investing proper resources in adaptive student-centric testing, teachers, students, parents, and the taxpayers making the investment will have the benefit of a more accountable system.

I do have serious worries, however, about the ability of our most rural and poor students to benefit from this new learning tool. Schools in rural, high-poverty areas with lower internet bandwidths (as discussed in an earlier chapter) will not have the capacity to allow their students to take full advantage of new learning technologies to compete in the global marketplace. This is yet another reason why we must also address our infrastructure needs to increase broadband connectivity for *all* our children. But to further ensure rural schools' access we also have to make sure that federal government funding to schools for better broadband is not disproportionately focused on the number of students attending the school, and we should raise the permanent funding cap on the E-Rate program that provides federal funding to such schools for connectivity.[293][294]

Student Loans for Higher Education Should Not be a Debt Sentence

When President Eisenhower in 1958 pushed Congress to pass the first national legislation providing for student loans, he did so because he realized our national security depended on it.[295] The year before, the Soviets had launched their Sputnik satellite, marking the first step in the space race. Ike knew that if we were going to beat our greatest global competitor, we would need the brain-power to do it, and his National Defense Student Loan program would play a major role in training the engineers who would eventually help put a man on the moon. Achieving our common enterprise – leading the world in science, innovation, and imagination so that we all might reap the economic rewards – was only possible by empowering rugged individuals with raw talent to seek higher education and take us up to improbable heights.

Today, more than a half-century later, the student loan landscape has changed drastically. While all students seeking higher education (not just aspiring rocket scientists) have *access* to an expanded national student loan program, the *affordability* of higher education has dramatically diminished. As early as the 1990s, this problem was evident: a GAO study found that between 1980 and 1995, the average tuition at four-year public colleges increased 234 percent while, in comparison, median household income had only increased 82 percent.[296]

Since the study, this trend unfortunately has continued, with tuition rising 73 percent from 1999 to 2009 and with median family income falling by 7 percent.[297] What this means is that the cost of higher education has eaten up an ever-increasing percentage of family income, forcing more and more students to borrow beyond what their family can sacrifice. Shockingly, today there are 40 million Americans with at least one open student loan. Total student loan debt is at a daunting $1.2 trillion dollars[298] with an average debt of $29,400 for bachelor's degree graduates.[299] At $1.2 trillion, student loan debt accounts for more debt than America's auto loans and credit cards, and is the largest source of debt for households aside from mortgages.[300]

As a result of being saddled with such a high cost for education, the Federal Reserve Bank of New York has found that today's graduates take longer to purchase homes, are significantly less likely to buy a car, and contribute less to overall consumer spending.[301] Such evidence shows that these historic levels of student loan debt aren't only a burden on graduates, but on our entire economy.

Worse yet, new small business creation – the backbone of our economy – is negatively affected by the increasing level of loan debt. An analysis by the Federal Reserve Bank of Philadelphia and the University of Pennsylvania found a "significant and economically meaningful negative correlation between changes in student loan debt and net business formation" for small businesses with one to four employees.[302]

The debt has even become a burden on the American family itself. Parents across Pennsylvania have confirmed to me anecdotally what new data proves to be true: over a third of the "Millennial" generation – 21.6 million people age 18 to 31 – are living with their parents.[303] And while there isn't yet a completely clear causal connection between the student debt rate and the increasing age at which young people decide to get married and have children, data shows at least a strong correlation.[304]

The crisis is clear. But thus far, our leaders have failed to fully address the growing student loan bubble. Their failures have been two-fold. First, we need to address *both* sides of the college affordability equation – federal aid *and* accountability from colleges for skyrocketing costs. Our leaders have focused heavily on how to structure federal aid with too little focus on the drastic increase in the sticker prices of institutions of higher education. Second, when our leaders have tried to address the federal aid end of the equation, they keep using the wrong yardsticks.

The College Accountability Side of the Equation

Colleges across the country have for decades failed to hold themselves accountable to their students for providing an education at a reasonable premium. In Pennsylvania, I am proud to say that we have the third most colleges and universities of any state in America – over 250. At the same time, however, I am concerned that the University of Pittsburgh and Penn State University place number one and number two on the nationwide list for highest in-state tuition for four-year public colleges or universities.[305] Worse yet, fifteen of Penn State's branch campuses are also in the top five percent for cost, as is

Temple University in Philadelphia. While a significant portion of the recent tuition price hikes in Pennsylvania have come from the State's education cuts, simply blaming just the former governor and the State Legislature misses a more important point.

The truth is that too many colleges and universities are notoriously bad at managing costs and are accustomed to simply passing expenses along to students in the form of higher tuition and fees. A variety of factors are at play here. At many schools, the faculty teaching load has gradually declined over the years with full professors at some universities teaching only one or two classes a year. Additionally, colleges and universities use shared governance models where power and authority is vested in people (faculty without business credentials) who are not accountable to economics in times when finances are tight and changes must be made.

Because colleges and universities have failed to rein in costs over the last three decades, the federal government has been forced to increase grants, loans, and other forms of aid. And families' willingness to pay these steep tuition increases that frequently exceeded the Consumer Price Index has also been helped by federal education tax credits and deductions. Looking at the numbers, I believe we are far beyond the tipping point. This does not mean we should stop giving grants, loans, aid, credits, and deductions to students and their families; rather, it means that it's time to start holding colleges and universities accountable for their costs because they can't do it themselves.

The solution isn't to cut government aid to students and their families; the solution is long-overdue accountability from the higher education community. Drastic steps may be necessary. I believe the time has come for conditioning government loan money to colleges and universities upon the institution's transparent accountability in tuition and fees being at or below inflation. We still want students to be able to select the best school they can achieve, but we must simultaneously ensure schools no longer saddle 18 year olds with decades of debt caused by inefficiency and inflexibility. We need a lot more sunshine and a lot more transparency.

A Loan Interest Rate that Works

Moving on to the government loan side of the equation, we need interest rates that are predictable for families, affordable for students, and reliable to the taxpayer. Currently, student loan rates are set on a year-by-year basis with the 10-year Treasury note rate as the base security, plus a certain percentage based on the type of loan given.[306] In 2014, direct loans for undergraduates had a 4.66 percent interest rate, unsubsidized graduate or professional loans were at 6.21 percent, and PLUS loans (for parents of graduate or professional students) were at 7.21 percent. That's an increase from 2013 when rates were 3.86 percent, 5.41 percent, and 6.41 percent, respectively.[307] And according to a CBO report based on anticipated loan rates under this equation, the government will make $127 billion in profits from student loans in the next decade as students continue to drown in debt.[308]

And yet, our legislators are at a philosophical impasse as to how to remedy the rate. On the one hand, you have Congressmen and Senators who see education as just another commodity in the market and want the government to stop subsidizing student loans entirely, leaving it to the private sector. On the other hand, others want student loans set at the same rate the Federal Reserve gives to big banks, which would be a little less than 1 percent.

I believe both sides are wrong. The proponents of private sector rates are wrong because they want students to pay double-digit market interest rates, and see education solely as a benefit to the individual – not our shared common enterprise. The other side is wrong here because the Federal Reserve's rate to banks is meant for extremely short-term deposits that ensure liquidity in our entire financial sector. Also, banks are backed by assets while a student is not, which is another sound reason the rates are lower. While we want to empower individual students to pursue years of education at a reasonable rate, our common enterprise requires that they at least have some skin in the game to pay back our taxpayer investment. Plus, by making near-no-interest loans to students, colleges and universities can keep increasing their prices on tuition.

We need a better equation that takes into account a variety of factors: 1) our national need to invest in knowledge; 2) the dual premises that the government shouldn't be in the business of making money from students, but that students should bear a reasonable burden for the risk incurred; and 3) a student's cost of living at the time of the loan. Therefore, we need a better base security that is more reflective of the term of a student loan, and we need a consumer-driven economic instrument to determine what we "add" to the base security rate instead of just picking a percentage.

Accordingly, we need to first determine the base. To do so, we have to understand the data on loan lengths.

The average student loan takes 13.4 years to repay (up from 7.4 years in 1992).[309] While many students take less than 13.4 years, there are many students who take up to 25 years to repay their loans.[310] So, the fact that we currently use a 10-year Treasury note as the base security doesn't make sense given the length of time it takes to pay off these loans. Instead, we should use both the 10-year note and the 30-year note to account more accurately for the disparity in loan repayment times, with each base representing one-half of the base interest rate. Using 2014 numbers to calculate the base, we would have a 10-year note at 1.85 percent and a 30-year note at 3.04 percent – the average of which would be 2.45 percent as the base.

Now that we have a base (2.45 percent), we need an economic instrument to tell us what to add onto the base in order to account for changes in the cost of living. The percentage to "add" to the base should be one half of the annual percentage change in the Consumer Price Index (CPI) from the previous year. CPI reflects goods and services purchased for consumption by a population, like food, clothing, transportation, and the like. We already use CPI to determine cost of living adjustments for the military, social security, eligibility for food stamps, collective bargaining agreements, and various other items. CPI tells us what it costs students to live once they graduate, which makes sense to include as a portion of the student loan equation.

In 2013, the annual percentage change in CPI was 1.5 percent. So, adding half of the percentage change in CPI (.75 percent) to the loan base (2.45 percent) would result in a 3.2 percent fixed rate for student loans. For post-graduate level loans, the formula can be reconfigured to reflect the extra years of schooling and the longer repayment period. To do so, the base would be adjusted with the 30 year Treasury note accounting for 75 percent of the base rate while the 10 year note constitutes 25 percent. A sliding scale could be developed from a one year masters to a three year law degree to an eight year doctorate.

I believe this equation is superior to the current model, as well as the alternatives that are being proposed by each side. It is less than today's rate, but it is based on a capital return on investment timeline. The demand for higher education is only going to grow as the postsecondary degree becomes the new high school diploma. This formula balances our common purpose need for an educated and innovative next generation while empowering the rugged individuals of tomorrow to be all they can be.

A Need for National Service

For a long time I have been convinced that America would benefit greatly from all youth participating in national service programs, and it is something that I have advocated since I entered public life almost a decade ago. In teaching Pennsylvania's youth for the last three years as a college and law school professor, I was every day amazed and inspired by their ability to take on old problems with new eyes and cast aside the obsolete dogmas of my own generation. But what they lack, I believe, is a shared common experience to bind them together and a sense of having a real stake in their country.

What I don't believe is that a national service program should be in significant part through the military. The five service branches can provide one of many options, but the fact is that when the military (and the taxpayers) make an investment in training, it has to be long term – at least a three year commitment after one year of training. Today's military is so high-tech that it can often take a year to get to the fleet. Some may choose to go this route, but for most there are other options. When I talk about national service, I envision programs as diverse as Teach for America, AmeriCorps, and everything the nonprofit sector has to offer.

I believe this is crucial because our national dialogue has been too divisive. We need a sense of fellowship in this country where we can disagree as individuals and still join together in a common enterprise. During my time in the Navy, officers often disagreed but came together to make a decision and move forward. Universal national service would provide a national esprit de corps that ties the country together in a time of great division, because each person has served their nation.

At the 2012 Aspen Ideas Festival, retired Army General Stan McChrystal laid out the philosophical foundation for a national service program in words that I often reference across Pennsylvania. He said that "if every person that's age 25 and older meets and the first question is 'hey, where'd you serve? What did you do?' If that's the start of the conversation, I think it would be really powerful."[311] With 600,000 applications to AmeriCorps' 80,000 positions and 150,000 applications requests for Peace Corps 4,000 positions, McChrystal said this disparity "represents democratic energy wasted and a generation of patriotism needlessly squandered."[312]

We already are able to ascertain the budgetary return on investment for national service, and there is strong evidence that it is a worthy taxpayer investment. A study by the Center for Benefit-Cost Studies at Columbia University found that while the taxpayer cost of our current national service programs is $1.7 billion annually, the total social benefit of the output produced and long-term gains is $6.5 billion.[313] That means taxpayers are seeing almost a $4 return for every $1 invested. What is unclear, however, is whether that return would increase or decrease under a *universal* service program that I am advocating. Our leaders should commit to further non-partisan analysis of the cost of such a program, and be open to investing to the furthest extent that cost-benefit studies allow. We need to do the right assessment, but we need to do it properly.

I am well aware that my position on this issue may not be very popular. According to recent polling, 71 percent of voters oppose mandatory national service.[314] That's no surprise – we all want to be rugged individuals and serve the country in our own way. But that is exactly what a robust national service program would look like. Between traditional government programs and nonprofit creativity, every young man and woman should be able to find their own unique way to serve our common enterprise. This is a program that I truly believe in, and it is incumbent upon leaders to convince the people that their vision is not only possible but preferable to the status quo. I look forward to continuing this campaign in the coming years and working with others to show the value of a society where everybody – not just principally those of us who wore a uniform – can say "I served my country."

Chapter 12

CONTINUED GLOBAL LEADERSHIP FOR SECURITY AND PROSPERITY

I was incredibly blessed to have had a 31-year career in the United States Navy before going into elected office. For much of my time in uniform, I was thousands of miles away from home, spanning a period from the midst of the Cold War to the post-September 11 world. As I served our country overseas, I saw the ways in which events far from Pennsylvania, both big and small, impacted our lives at home. I learned how other countries' policies, the way that those countries behaved, or how they chose to compete in a global economy mattered to our security and our economic prosperity.

So, when I arrived in Congress, my experience had already taught me that we as Americans cannot tackle our problems or challenges here at home without also thinking about what is happening around the world. I have always been a firm believer that American leaders have a responsibility to explain this connection – between the foreign and domestic – to their constituents.

Today, there's a need for American leaders to take this responsibility even more seriously, as the world is going through profound changes that will require our country to remain engaged – and to be a leader on the world stage as much, if not more so, than we have been for the past century. America needs to be engaged with the world not because we are hungry for needless overseas adventures – but because our safety, our jobs, our economy, and our future prosperity depend on it.

I fully understand that many Americans – after a decade of wars that drained our treasury and readiness, strained our alliances, and in many ways left us more vulnerable – are tired and want to turn inward and focus solely on affairs here at home. But the truth is that, in this globalized and increasingly competitive world, meaningful domestic policies must respond to global challenges.

Yes, this applies in a traditional, national security sense – we need to keep ourselves safe from foreign threats. But, in the face of growing international economic competition, it increasingly also applies to our economic security. For our economy to thrive in the long run, with good jobs, successful companies, and a solid tax base – without which we cannot pay for our own defense – American leaders need to lead and marshal our diplomatic power to push for a world that is fair for our workers, open to our businesses both large and small, and respectful of our ideas and innovation.

Other countries such as Brazil, China, Germany, and Japan are looking outward – mindful that their physical and economic security are codependent – advocating for their companies and fighting for their interests. We cannot afford not to do the same. Instead of fanning the flames of isolationism, we need leaders who can write a smart national security strategy for the 21st century – a strategy that will enable us to respond not only to many of the traditional issues that we have faced since the end of the Second World War, but also to new challenges that have emerged from the changing geopolitical conditions in recent years.

As we work together as a nation to advance our national interests in the coming decades, we must ask ourselves: What does it mean for America to continue to lead and embrace the world in a responsible manner, and why does that matter to our well-being here at home? How do we respond to different kinds of challenges effectively? And, where should we focus our precious resources and efforts going forward to advance our national interests?

Our World Today and the Meaning of America's Engagement

In today's interconnected world, the truth is that America can fully thrive as an individual nation only if the whole of nations are able to pursue prosperity in a stable and free world – where countries behave in a way that contributes to long-term peace and development, respect the rights of their citizens, and honor the rules of the road that have kept the world safe since the end of World War II.

Indeed, over the last 70 years, we have made tremendous sacrifices working toward that world. We stood firm with Europe as it rebuilt in the aftermath of a devastating world war. We maintained stability and kept sea-lanes open in the Asia-Pacific so that nations in the region could trade and thrive. We promoted freedom and democracy abroad even as we fought a painful and continuous battle for justice and equality here at home.

We have made our share of mistakes in our attempts to build that better world. But what makes America exceptional is that we have always been guided not by pure power politics but by an ideal and a sense of obligation as a great power: that if we want to benefit from a peaceful and prosperous world, then we must do our part to keep it and advance it – recognizing that our own wealth and security have a stake in it.

This must continue in our own time.

Today, as in the past, our challenges are global. We face geopolitical and economic competition from China, threats of instability in the Asian waters, Russian aggression in Ukraine, bitter conflict between the Israelis and Palestinians, security threats to our interests in Libya, civil war in Syria, continued unrest in Iraq as well as in Africa, global climate change, and terrorism challenging civil societies around the world.

But, unlike the past, what complicates matters for us today is the fact that none of the challenges that I just mentioned fit into any single geographical area, neat issue-specific box, or friend-or-foe matrix. Yes, it may be easier to make sense of the world if our choices were simply black or white, good or evil, home or abroad – like the way things were during the Cold War. But we are living in quite a different context. We are living in a gray world, a transnational world, with no clear division, where every challenge, however far, is a home game. Read the newspapers, turn on the news, and you will see plenty of examples.

Let us start with something that is still fresh on the minds of most Americans: terrorism. Almost a decade and a half after September 11, the global war on terror is not over. Non-state actors, sometimes acting alone, sometimes as part of well-networked groups, continue to pose a threat to our infrastructure, electrical grids, water supply, cities, and all forms of travel. This is true not only in the United States, but around the world.

Terrorism is not something that we can fight by mobilizing mass armies. There are no specific countries we can target. It is about coordination and cooperation – with friends and allies, to be sure, but also with countries that we may not particularly like. It is about gathering information diligently, wherever we can find it, and sharing that intelligence so we can stay one step ahead of those who want to do us harm, and contain their ability to operate.

One of the most challenging terrorist groups to surface since al Qaeda is the Islamic State of Iraq and Syria, or ISIS, which is a 20,000-person group that commands influence over and terrorizes a large swath of land in an unstable Iraq and Syria.[315] ISIS is brutal and well-resourced. Its members have killed innocent people, including Americans. And, perhaps most worrisome, ISIS has demonstrated an ability to attract and recruit people from around the world – including Americans – to fight for its causes.[316] These recruits could potentially return to their home countries and carry out attacks. For that reason, ISIS poses a serious threat to the domestic security of the United States. No responsible American leader can afford not to confront them.

If we do nothing, if we do not work with other nations to beat back ISIS's attempt to overrun Iraq – still fragile after a decade of war – we face the risk of seeing Iraq turn into a lawless space from which the well-funded extremist group could operate freely as a base where they will be able to plan attacks against our homeland and our allies elsewhere.

So the President was right when he decided to lead an international coalition, including Middle Eastern nations, to contain ISIS. This will be a long-term effort – not unlike fighting cancer – with limited, targeted, and defined air strikes and to provide arms and training for the Iraqi government in order to boost its ability to counter the threats posed by this terrorist organization.

Ultimately, though, the American military will not be the final solution for Iraq to eliminate ISIS and solidify stability for itself; the solution will be a political one that the Iraqis will settle for themselves, where all sides, Sunnis and Shias, can share power, respect the country's constitution, and together build a viable, independent nation capable of ensuring its own security.

But the United States can play a leading role by bringing together different stakeholders – in the region and around the world – in order to halt the advance of this violent extremist group, and provide some breathing space for Iraqis to bring some measure of stability back to their own country.

One of the stakeholders in all this, of course, is the next-door neighbor, Iran, a country that obviously has a strong interest in a stable Iraq. Even as we work hard to stop Iran's nuclear ambitions, we have to address the fact that that they could potentially play a useful role in promoting a more peaceful region, even if it is for Iran's own self-interest.

So while recognizing our difficult history with Iran – they have, after all, called us "The Great Satan" – we also should not hesitate to use diplomacy to resolve the nuclear issue, and to ensure its leaders respect international law. Perhaps, along the way, we may be able to see how both of our countries can contribute to long-term stability in the Middle East.

Beyond Iran, if we move about 1,500 miles westward, we will bring ourselves to one of the most seemingly intractable disputes in the world today: between the Israelis and Palestinians. This historical problem has layers of grievances and a fair share of dashed hopes, conflicts, and short wars. But however deep the resentment may run between the two sides, this is an issue that the United States simply cannot ignore, for continued violence and destruction would only breed yet another generation of hatred, some of which will inevitably be directed toward us.

Israel has the absolute right to exist as a state, and we must continue to stand strongly beside it to ensure its security. Its people are entitled to pursue their own happiness without having to fear missiles falling onto their streets. Its people should not have to worry about their soldiers being kidnapped, or tunnels that undermine their safety and security. Israel is a beacon of democracy in the region, a leader in innovation, and a driver of economic growth – if Israel is not secure, neither will be the broader Middle East nor the United States.

And yet, it is also true that Israel may be safe but will not be secure until there is a peaceful resolution with its Palestinian and Arab neighbors. I believe we have no alternative but to strive for a two-state solution, where both Israelis and Palestinians are able to have homelands to call their own. But for us to reach that goal, we also need leaders on both sides – and throughout the region and the world – who are committed to the cause of peace.

The United States must actively reach out to and remain engaged with all stakeholders, including the leaders of Jordan, Egypt, and Turkey, to find a sensible way forward. Forty years ago, Egyptian President Anwar Sadat asserted a leadership role in the region and charted a new course in its relations with Israel that continues to move the world. Will we find our generation's Anwar Sadat? That, in many ways, should be the key question guiding our efforts in finding a lasting solution between the two sides.

Finally, if entrenched conflicts and terrorism are not enough to show the importance of being flexible and practical-minded as we deal with the interconnectedness of this complex world, consider the matter of global public health. Even as nations jealously guard their borders, we cannot deny the inconvenient fact that, in the age of jet travel, infectious diseases could spread easily, and in an instant endanger the health and even lives of citizens living in New York and Lagos, London and Rio de Janeiro, Tehran and Melbourne, Tokyo and Moscow. Deadly viruses know no boundaries, and our solutions must go beyond geography.

So even our health experts and researchers have to dive into foreign affairs – and in their work they are often called upon to share expertise, knowledge, and best practices with their counterparts around the world to coordinate disease prevention and control the spread of viruses. The Ebola outbreak in Africa should have taught us that lesson, reminding us that we have no choice but to keep looking outward, even as we protect our interests here at home.

And then there is the strategic center of gravity for America in this century – the western Pacific, and China. Its challenges are many – from economic and diplomatic to financial and security – and in the pages that follow, they will be fully addressed, for it is in Asia that so much of our overall security will be determined.

So that's the world in which we live today.

Our current challenges are often transnational in nature, crossing borders and requiring innovative thinking on our part to cooperate with other governments when we can, secure support from Non-Governmental Organizations who can help, share intelligence when appropriate, issue economic sanctions when the time is right, and use our military wisely if and when we must.

A Smart National Security Strategy for Today

I know what I just said can be a discomforting fact for many Americans: that there is no set answer to, and certainly no one-dimensional way to think about, the challenges that we face. Our solutions will come in different shapes and sizes, sometimes a combination of our available assets and resources – depending on what needs to be done.

In some ways, I would like to think that this is similar to building a good tool kit, capable of responding to different tasks with the right set of tools. Our kit needs to be diverse, so we have at our disposal the tools we need to tackle a full spectrum of issues, such as, among others:

- Maintaining a strong and globally competitive economic base at home;
- Fighting al Qaeda and terrorism;
- Arresting the spread of deadly diseases;
- Saving lives in natural disasters afar;
- Addressing the impact of climate change;
- Promoting economic development overseas;

- Pursuing a lasting solution for peace in the Middle East;
- Checking Russia; and,
- Addressing China.

We need, in other words, a *smart* national security strategy to deal with such a diversity and range of challenges. By "smart," I mean we have to confront our challenges in a way that fits the needs of this increasingly complicated, ever more connected and sophisticated world.

A smart national security strategy capable of addressing the wide array of challenges that I described above will consist of five major categories:

1. **Enhance diplomatic engagement** in order to maintain reliable allies and partners to help us address problems that arise around the world;
2. **Advance economic partnerships** to promote stable growth and development overseas, opening up opportunities for American companies, investments, and, in particular, new markets to sell American-made goods and products;
3. **Maintain a strong, flexible military** capable of undergirding our global diplomatic and economic efforts and addressing the diverse set of challenges in the coming decades;
4. **Be able to weigh well the costs and benefits if the decision arises of "when and why" to use military force** that would send our men and women into combat; and,
5. **Prioritize our resources and efforts** to reflect the increasingly important role that Asia plays in geopolitics and the global economy.

Enhance Diplomatic Engagement

The first and perhaps primary component of a smart national security strategy is to ensure that the United States is always at the table, leading and driving the conversations among our allies and partners on the most important developments around the world. We are a global nation with security and economic interests in every corner. As such, we need an active, engaged, and well-resourced diplomatic agenda to make sure that we are always present, advancing our interests.

An important part of this diplomatic agenda is to ensure that we maintain the trust and support of our key allies and partners around the world. At a time when challenges are increasingly global and transnational in nature, and at a time when our nation, like so many nations, is facing budgetary constraints, we need the help of our friends to preserve peace and stability in the world so that we can grow and prosper along with it. So when a rogue nation challenges international law, or when terrorist organizations disrupt civil societies at home or abroad, we can work collectively to stop them.

Our cooperation with European nations to counter Russia's aggressive behavior toward its neighbors is an important example. President Vladimir Putin knows that Russia is in a difficult position. Longing to regain the sphere of influence that Russia lost at the end of the Cold War, and mindful of its long-term demographic decline which will dent its geopolitical and economic significance,[317] Putin wants to use this moment of opportunity to secure, while he still can, what he believes to be Russia's national interest.

In doing so, Putin has shown a willingness to violate international law and the sovereignty of independent nations,[318] disrupt regional peace and order, violate the freedoms and rights of Russian citizens,[319] and extort neighboring countries and European nations who challenge his behavior by manipulating the gas market.[320] Unfortunately, as we saw in the downing of the Malaysian Airlines flight over the skies of Ukraine, Putin's actions have had tragic and destabilizing consequences.

Our response to Russia at this time will not involve the use of force. It will require us, instead, to leverage all of our diplomatic and economic power to isolate it from a community of nations that understands the value of preserving a rules-based and respectful global order. Our leaders must continue to apply pressure on the Russian government to force it to change its behavior by reaffirming and strengthening our alliances with European nations. For we cannot do this alone – we need our allies' help to enhance sanctions against Moscow as well as Putin's key political and business associates, freeze their global assets, and block banking transactions. For our response to be effective, we need our allies' and partners' "buy-in" to ensure that the international community will not tolerate disruptions to existing international norms – norms that have kept Europe safe, stable, and prosperous since the end of the Second World War.

What we can do at this time is take advantage of the fact that so much of Russia's power and leverage comes from its status as Europe's gas station. More than any of our various economic sanctions, the dynamics of the international hydrocarbon market have hurt Russia the most. That's because crude oil and oil products comprise nearly half of Russia's budget revenues, and Russia's overall budget assumes $100 a barrel oil prices.[321] The recent drop in the cost of a barrel of oil – precipitated by record U.S. production and steady Saudi output – caused a steep decline in the value of the ruble and has evaporated a considerable portion of the Russian government's budget. Energy is an economic weapon, and we must be willing to wield it appropriately in our array of security options against aggression.

Beyond countering Russian aggression, though, our leaders must think more broadly about the significance of our alliances with European nations. Most notably, as we formulate our national security policies for the next century, a time when rising authoritarian regimes around the world are seeking to challenge an American-led, rules-based global system that has, by and large, kept the world away from large-scale war for decades, we have no better allies than our European partners. The United States and Europe have a shared interest in promoting universal values – human rights, democracy, good governance, and the rule of law. We recognize that we can only be successful in advancing these values at home if we live in a world that also lives by them. For the sake of a peaceful 21st century, America must lead, but our European partners also need to do more to ensure the viability of a rules-based global system from which all nations can benefit.

Advance Economic Partnerships

The second pillar for building a smart national security strategy is the idea that fostering balanced economic development and promoting economic partnerships will be just as important as, if not a prerequisite for, maintaining security.

Africa provides one of the most appropriate and clearest illustrations. Throughout much of my lifetime, Africa had too often been portrayed in the media as a war-torn land of poverty and diseases. But in the last decade or so, that narrative has been evolving. Of the ten fastest-growing economies in the world today, six of them are on that continent.[322] The growth rates of a number of African nations have, in recent years, actually exceeded China's.[323] There is a growing middle class in Africa, driving thriving new markets, ready and eager to become new consumers of American products.[324]

It was no surprise, then, that the United States has declared a renewed focus on Africa, charting a new approach in order to reflect new realities and opportunities. At the very first U.S.-Africa Leadership Summit, which was held in Washington in the summer of 2014, $900 million worth of deals were signed – an expectation that trade and commerce will increasingly define the African experience in this century.[325]

But Africa's continued growth, like everything else, is not guaranteed. They will need rule of law and independent courts to ensure that contracts are honored and workers are protected. They will need active civil society organizations to help keep official corruption in check. They will need open, transparent, and representative governments to ensure that hard-earned wealth is fairly distributed – not just the well connected or those who have control over the continent's coveted natural resources.

The United States has much to gain from a stronger, more prosperous Africa. We stand to benefit economically, to be sure, but a more productive and prosperous Africa will also make it a better partner in our efforts to fight terrorism and maintain regional security. For these reasons, I foresee our military command for that continent – AFRICOM – becoming not just a hub of activities for our armed forces, but also increasingly a central platform for all aspects of our national power. That's why AFRICOM's deputy commander is a civilian from the State Department, which is unique among our unified commands. This is altogether fitting because it allows us to find meaningful partnerships in Africa from aid projects to rule of law training programs to public health specialists.

But serious challenges remain for Africa, and new ones are rising. For example, no other continent will be impacted more greatly by climate change than Africa.[326] Many African countries' already-severe problems with hunger, drought, and malaria could only get worse – and the areas at risk will only grow larger.

Many African nations have bright futures, with promising opportunities for all. But their security will increasingly be dependent on trade and robust economic growth; and growth can only be continued if the continent is peaceful and stable. We can do our part in facilitating their success by helping to nurture reliable and enduring institutions. That must be our approach to Africa going forward – a smart strategy that understands the natural connection between security and development.

Of course, Africa is not alone in demonstrating what America has to gain from building meaningful economic partnerships. Latin America, a region that we have given short shrift for much too long – and much to our own economic detriment – also promises to be a key area of opportunity for the United States in the coming decades. Countries such as Brazil, Chile, Colombia, Peru, and

Uruguay have become economic powerhouses of the region. In fact, over a one-third of the population in Latin America can now be considered "middle class" – ready, and perhaps eager, to buy more of our goods.[327] Many of them are not only keen consumers of American products, they are also increasingly outward-looking, traveling to other countries, including here – their influential neighbor to the north. To put some of this growth into perspective, in the last ten years, Brazil had lifted almost 40 million people out of poverty.[328]

We must continue to promote greater trade relations and exchanges with our Latin American partners. By doing so, perhaps we can encourage regional leaders to tackle some of the much-needed domestic changes and reforms in those countries – such as streamlining business and economic regulations and enhancing local infrastructure – to make their economies more competitive. By fostering greater American engagement there, we can play a positive role in driving further economic changes and development in the region, making them into more effective partners for the United States in regional security and economic affairs – beneficial for them and for us. And our opening with Cuba is a strong step in this direction – for our economic trade and security.

Using the power of economic cooperation to create more effective partnerships is something we must also do in our strategic center of gravity – the Asian Pacific – and this will be addressed further below.

Maintain a Flexible and Credible Military

Third, a smart strategy to engage the world will require us to rethink the ways in which our armed forces fit within our national security policy. In the coming decades, when it comes to how we use our military as we defend and safeguard our interests abroad, we need to focus our strategic thinking on force *posture*, not force *structure*.

What do I mean by that?

For far too long, we have benchmarked our military might to the size of our forces, believing that the number of ships, airways, and brigades is what matters – just like during the Cold War. But, today, the strike capabilities of ten aircraft carriers and their enhanced technological airwings are about equal to 90 aircraft carriers fifteen years ago. So, knowing this, should we continue to be obsessed with size and numbers?

The right metric in our time, the smart metric, is knowledge. And knowledge is the fundamental metric on which our national security should be based. Then comes the speed and agility with which we can respond because we are aware of "what to do" due to our knowledge. Specifically:

- Are we acquiring the right information-based systems – particularly through the domain of cyberspace – to provide us the knowledge we need to have?
- And have we also nurtured the right talents and provided the appropriate intellectual training to out-think our adversaries of all types?
- In a time when attacks could come at us in various ways (a terrorist bomb or cyber intrusions) and from different actors (a nation-state or an extremist group), what are the other kinds of smart technology for the speed and agility that we will need in order to stay ahead of the threats of our

time – on land, at sea, in the air, and in cyberspace to take advantage of our knowledge?

I have been wrestling with these questions for quite some time. As a naval officer, my final assignment was serving as Deputy Chief of Naval Operations. In that position, I was responsible for helping the Navy think through and develop its war fighting needs for the future, starting with the next five-year period. We were innovative in developing and acquiring the right warfare systems, but we did it by constantly asking ourselves to think about what the future warfare environment would look like.

As a result, in 2005, the Navy sent Congress a shipbuilding plan that vastly improved its capability to win a future conflict by investing in knowledge and speed – a force *posture*, not just a more costly force *structure*. So rather than buying more submarines at $2 billion each, the plan proposed a netted sensor information system to track enemy underwater movements, and then direct an aircraft or drone to drop a torpedo for the "kill."

Our investment in force posture with the newest sensors for more rapid knowledge acquisition, our efforts to enhance our ability to quickly turn just-gathered intelligence into swift action, and our continued development of aircraft technologically connected to exact targeting information can replace large, costly force structures. They can help in missions as diverse as determining the precise location of Osama bin Laden to tracking any of North Korea's aggressive moves.

This makes national security sense, and it is also fiscally responsible – exactly the kind of forward-thinking, smart policy that we need. We need to posture our different forces in line to maximize the benefits of new technology, not how we structured them in the past as large organizations – a numbers game made for a different, more rigid time that has certainly passed.

Be Able to Explain the Cost and Benefit of When and Why we Need to Use Force

The fourth pillar of a smart national security strategy requires our leaders to carefully assess and explain, when necessary, the reasons for which we need to deploy our military. For all the talk of preparing our military for 21st century challenges, the truth remains that our military stands in the back, undergirding and supporting all other aspects of our national power – political, diplomatic, and economic. If there comes a time when we have no other option but to send our troops into harm's way, the American President has a responsibility to justify and explain, very clearly, his or her reasoning to the American people.

Whether and how to go to war is dictated predominately by our national interests. When I served as Director of Defense Policy on President Clinton's National Security Council in the 1990s, I helped develop a comprehensive strategy for our engagement overseas, defining our national interests into three separate categories.

- First and foremost are our "vital interests," those having to do with the very survivability of America, for which we will do anything.
- Second are our "important interests," where a change in the character or well-being of the world would affect the United States importantly.

- Third are "humanitarian interests" that align with our ideals.

For any commitment by our leaders to engage our military and defend our national interests, as defined above, it will require:

- A clearly defined, achievable mission, with the use of military force carefully matched to the political objective;
- An assessment of potential benefits weighed against the risks and costs – both human and financial – to the American people;
- A pre-established timeline and specific, quantifiable milestones to reveal the extent of progress;
- In every case, contingency plans must be put in place if our goals are not being met and we must adjust. And, a viable exit strategy must be available, whether the operation in question is failing or succeeding.

This engagement strategy was ignored by the George W. Bush administration in Iraq that seemed to view careful assessment as an indication of uncertainty or "dithering" and, at times, to value politics over pragmatism. To me, the bottom line will always be: if there is a plan to address problems facing our nation, particularly if it involves the use of military force, leaders must be willing and able to show definitively why up front.

No matter what the challenge, the American people want to know where we are going, why, and how we will get there. The question of how long it will take and what it will cost must be answered up front. They want to know if the plan is working. And if it is not, they want to know that we will have the courage to change course. Any proposal must have measurable benchmarks. And leaders must be held accountable for meeting those benchmarks. We need such accountability from our leaders – especially if we are going to commit our treasury and the lives of those willing to serve in uniform.

Prioritize our Resources and Efforts

Finally, a smart national security strategy will also require us to make smart choices. The fact that we have challenges around the world does not mean that we have to focus equally on every problem everywhere – that is neither practical nor wise. We must hone in on the ones that would impact our lives and interests the most in the long run.

In every generation, developments around the world – often beyond our control – compel our nation to focus on particular issues or regions. So even as global challenges abounded, our security and economic interests required us to prize Europe's economic recovery after the Second World War, lock our attention on the Soviet Union during the Cold War, and dedicate our resources toward anti-terrorism efforts after September 11. In my own lifetime, our country had shifted its focus from Europe to the Soviet Union to the Middle East, and must now increasingly do so to the Western Pacific.

It is clear that in the first half of the 21st century, a significant share of America's security and economic interests will be in the Asia Pacific, a region that hosts some of the world's most dynamic, influential, vibrant, and rapidly changing countries: Japan, Australia, South Korea, Indonesia, Vietnam, and, of course, China.[329]

For all these reasons, in our time, a smart national security strategy will naturally require us to enhance our focus on the Asia Pacific region. Whether our nation can maintain its economic competitiveness in a peaceful and stable world will largely depend on how well – and how intelligently – we use our diverse national security tool kit to manage and secure our interests there.

Challenge and Opportunity of Our Time: The Asia Pacific

When we explain to the American people why a smart national security strategy should compel us to engage actively with the Asia Pacific region in the coming decades, and the reasons for which our security and economic well-being are at stake, we should lay out the following facts:

- Six of the world's top 20 economies are in the region – with the second and third biggest, China and Japan, looming large. As a whole, the Asia Pacific commands almost 60 percent of the world's GDP and about one-third of all world trade;[330]
- Eight years from now, 54 percent of the world's middle class will be found in the Asia Pacific, and the region will be responsible for over 40 percent of all middle class spending in the world;[331]
- Given the growing middle class, it was not surprising that, in 2012, the region bought about $4 trillion worth of goods and products from the world. By 2022, the number will rise to about $10 trillion.[332] It is a fast-growing market, with growing

spending power, and many will want our brand –
"made with quality in the USA."

- And indeed, our country is already benefiting
  from Asia's vibrant economies: last year,
  American exports to the region supported more
  than three million jobs here in the United States.[333]
  Our government has said that every $1 billion of
  exports translate to about 5,000 American jobs.[334]

For all this, it is very easy to understand our country's
rationale for setting a goal three years ago to double the
amount of U.S. exports within five years[335] – and Asia is
a big part of this equation.

And yet, as promising as these figures may be, we
cannot forget that some of the most vexing challenges
that we will face in the next few decades are in the Asia
Pacific. In order to leverage successfully the region's
growth to our country's benefit, we will need to be very
effective in advancing our national interests there.

A Stable Asia Pacific that Benefits America

From the American perspective, we want to ensure that
the region remains stable so that all nations, including
our own, can pursue prosperity and thrive in peace. More
than 90 percent of trade (by volume) transits through the
Asia Pacific by water.[336] Obviously, maritime security
is a source of concern, especially since various nations
are locked in heated territorial contests – with China
acting in a particularly aggressive manner in recent
years, unilaterally occupying disputed islands and
claiming waters that under international law fall under
the jurisdictions of other nations.[337] One accident, one

mistake by any country could set off a chain reaction with uncertain consequences. Any disruption to trade over there would certainly harm our economy over here.

That's why so many leaders in that region have openly asked our country to remain engaged in the Asia Pacific. They want Washington to be at the table when diplomats in the region are resolving their disagreements – to guide the discussions and act as an honest broker. They trust us not because of blind faith in America, but because we have a track record of keeping the peace there. The Asia Pacific region was able to thrive after the Second World War because America's military kept the peace, and our diplomats helped write the rules of the road that enabled countries to trade and prosper. These nations have seen our contributions, and they want that to continue.

A China that Must Play by the Rules

Our allies and partners in the Asia Pacific also increasingly worry about China's growing influence – which is understandable, given Beijing's rapidly developing economy and growing defense spending. So these nations, many of whom are our treaty allies (Australia, Japan, the Philippines, South Korea, and Thailand), expect us to show up and to lay out the terms defining the ways in which responsible nations should behave. And they want us to play a leadership role in bringing or pushing China into a global, rules-based system. China will need to understand that, as the world's second largest economy, it will have responsibilities far greater than most other nations – to uphold international law and the rules of global trade.

For all these reasons, we need to ensure that China, probably our most significant competitor in the coming years, will conduct itself in a way that is expected of any global power. China must do its part in advancing long-term peace and stability in the region and around the world. China must abide by international rules and norms, from security matters to dispute resolution to human rights to trade, so that other countries will not be harmed by its actions.

China must behave as such not only because it is important to the interests of our friends and allies in the Asia Pacific, but also because it is important to us here at home, especially as it relates to the health of our long-term economic growth.

Americans must understand that intense discussions between our country's officials and their counterparts in China are not simply isolated practices of foreign policy. They are, in fact, opportunities for us to bat for our economic interests – for our jobs, for our companies, and for our own future.

All of us, whether or not we are interested in foreign affairs, have a stake in these conversations. When we press China to respect the rule of law, to be a responsible global power, and to uphold trade rules, we are doing so with our own economic and national interests in mind.

Here are a few concrete examples.

If China continues to intimidate its neighbors over disputed territories and refuses to offer greater transparency and explanation for its rapid military buildup, it could entice other Asia Pacific countries to respond in ways – such as further intensifying their own arms build-up – that could easily destabilize this important region for American interests.

If China does not enforce its labor laws, or recognize workers' right to strike or petition over low wages, or stop companies from running afoul of environmental regulations, then China is essentially subsidizing its own companies by making it cheaper for them to do business – putting our own workers at a disadvantage.

If China refuses to punish its companies and citizens who violate intellectual property rights, then that reduces our earnings and profits. A recent study showed that the international theft of American intellectual properties, much of it stemming from China, cost our economy over $300 billion every year.[338] That's about how much we export to the Asia Pacific every year, hurting American companies and costing us tens of thousands of jobs.

If China continues to discriminate against American companies operating in China, then that dents our businesses' competitiveness across the board. A number of American companies doing business in China have voiced concerns that they are increasingly being targeted for arbitrary investigations and deprived of due process under Chinese courts.[339] These companies are finding that they are being denied a level playing field within China.

Finally, in terms of our relationship with China, one of the areas about which I am most concerned is the extent to which that country has a monopoly on the rare earths mining industry. Rare earths are highly valuable to our 21st century economy, and they are used to manufacture some of our most popular consumer products – in your smart phone, rare earths elements make your glass displays harder, more durable. These elements also carry tremendous national security significance – rare earths are needed to produce the magnets that guide the bombs dropped by the U.S. Air Force.[340] Rare earths also hold the key to developing clean and renewable energy. In addition, the chemical element thorium, a by-product of rare earths mining, would allow us to build reactors that generate electricity without the buildup of radioactive byproducts.[341]

The worrisome reality is that almost all – about 97 percent – of rare earths elements currently come from China.[342] And Chinese leaders have not been shy about using that advantage as leverage in geopolitics. A few years ago, when China and Japan were locked in a heated territorial dispute, Beijing responded by blocking rare earths exports to Japan – causing wide-spread concern within the Japanese manufacturing sector and, understandably, global markets. This kind of vulnerability should concern all nations, including ours.[343]

We used to do a fair amount of rare earths mining here in the United States. In fact, at the height of our manufacturing era, we produced most of the world's rare earths. But over the last three decades, as China built up its own industry and the prices dropped, we phased out our mining operations in this country. To too many, the economics made sense: if the Chinese can do it cheaper, then why not?

Well, the prices might be cheaper, but the cost to our long-term economic independence and national security is also greater. In the coming years, our policymakers must work with the private sector to incentivize a rebirth of our rare earths industry. If we want to be a nation that can compete on the world stage on our own terms, then we better have greater foresight and plan accordingly.

No doubt, it is a competitive world out there. Many countries are, just like us, angling for competitive advantages in the race for prosperity in the Asia Pacific.

And we too must fight for our interests in a competitive world.

Fight for America in a Competitive World

Under the circumstances that I just described, looking inward and doing nothing is not an option for our great nation. And yet, at times, it seems as though we are doing just that.

Take, for example, our current discussions over the fate of the Export-Import Bank of the United States, better known as the ExIm Bank, that I raised in an earlier chapter. The ExIm Bank provides loans to American businesses, including many small businesses, to help them compete in overseas markets. Many of our competitors, such as China, Japan, and Germany, all have their own and bigger versions of this bank. At a time when so many countries are doing all they can to advocate for their businesses and workers in a competitive global environment, we are proposing to do the exact opposite: eliminate an 80-year-old bank that has helped American companies compete in every corner of the world. It is just one example of the ways in which an irresponsible desire among some in Congress to play political football in an election year could jeopardize our country's long-term ability to compete in the world.

The Bank's data show that it has supported at least 1.2 million private sector jobs since 2009, with 205,000 jobs in 2013 alone.[344] It lends much-needed funds to small businesses – which, as I have said many times, have created 70 percent of new jobs in previous economic recoveries. In 2013, almost 90 percent of the Bank's transactions involved small businesses in America.[345]

It is true that, in simple dollar terms, a vast amount of the Bank's funding went to big corporations such as Boeing, General Electric, and Bechtel, but these companies' products are by their nature expensive and therefore require more capital. Besides, one should not forget that many of the companies who supplied these large corporations are small businesses themselves.

The ExIm Bank is one small tool for our country's businesses to stay competitive in a global economy. It does not cost taxpayers anything, and in fact has generated interest income for the government. And yet, we have somehow painted it as an example of "crony capitalism" – worthy of demise. Perhaps one economist is right: what we are doing, in this instance at least, is the "economic equivalent of unilateral disarmament."[346]

America has never unilaterally disarmed – never in history. We must do better.

Preparing for the Consequences of Climate Change

Throughout this book I have intertwined environmental concerns, particularly climate change, for its impact on our economic, financial, and even defense security. This is because I view climate change absolutely and unequivocally as a national security issue. Unlike almost any other national security issue in degree and range, a changing climate is universally disruptive and strikingly unpredictable. The challenges we face from climate change in the coming years are wholly unfamiliar to the defense posture of the preceding decades – and for that matter the entirety of our civilized history. We must be prepared to meet these challenges head on for ourselves and throughout the wider world. We must seize the leadership role on this issue, for our nation, for our children, our economy, our security, our world.

Even the Department of Defense (DOD) acknowledges the implications of this new security paradigm. In its 2014 Quadrennial Defense Review, climate change is explicitly addressed as a "significant challenge" for the U.S. military which it anticipates can increase the "frequency, scale, and complexity of future missions."[347] This is not a "tree-hugger" issue; it is a call to arms.

Here at home, changes in sea level are already affecting our military preparedness. The Navy is even now replacing 14 piers for ship-repair at Naval Station Norfolk because the water level is rising so rapidly and we have to replace them now before they are overrun by an encroaching ocean.[348] For our broader domestic economy and infrastructure in the longer-term, our rail lines, roadways, and subway transit systems along the coasts will be imperiled or underwater, affecting our competitiveness and devastating communities.

For all of this and so much more, we must be prepared. But we must also be proactive in our leadership and communication of the true threat climate change poses to us – and take the needed action both at home and in concert with others abroad. We must decrease our own global carbon footprint, but we must also establish an international norm that nations can and should be rugged individuals in advancing their own economic growth, but our global common enterprise – a livable and climatically predictable planet where we can all prosper together – must be preserved and protected if we want any chance to do well for ourselves as individual nations.

There is no greater long-term strategic livable challenge to the quality of future generations' livelihoods than climate change.

History's Calling

In my career, I have served my country in many contexts – as a naval officer, legislator, and more recently, college professor. I have traveled the country and traversed the world; I have talked to Americans here at home and citizens from afar. One of the most valuable lessons that I have learned in my years of service is that nothing in history is inevitable. We did not become a great nation because we were destined to be a great nation. We became great because we worked at it, fought for it, and did our best to maintain it. Progress is delicate, and a nation's efforts to achieve it must be continuously perfected.

As complex and challenging as this century has already been and will remain, I have no doubt that we will continue to play our role as a global leader, shaping and building a rules-based order for the good of all, so long as we are willing to appreciate our deep connection to the world, engage with it as we always have, and marshal our resources to meet the needs of our time.

NOTES

Notes

Chapter 1

1. Galston, William A. "Declining Optimism Among the Obama Coalition." *The Brookings Institution.* 23 Sept. 2014. <http://www.brookings.edu/blogs/fixgov/posts/2014/09/23-american-values-survey-american-dream-galston>.

Chapter 2

2. "How Americans Define Success and Making It in the U.S. Today." *American Dream 2.0:* (2013). Learnvest and Chase Blueprint. <http://learnvest.cachefly.net/wp-content/uploads/2013/10/Chase_LV_AmericanDream.pdf>.
3. "State Economic Profiles." *Sba.gov.* U.S. Small Business Administration, n.d. Web. <https://www.sba.gov/category/advocacy-navigation-structure/research-and-statistics/state-economic-profiles>.
4. Haltiwanger, John C., Ron S. Jarmin, and Javier Miranda. "Who Creates Jobs? Small vs. Large vs Young." *NBER Working Paper Series* (2010): 1-51. *National Bureau of Economic Research.* <http://www.nber.org/papers/w16300.pdf>.

5. Id.
6. Lynn, Barry C., and Linda Khan. "The Slow-Motion Collapse of American Entrepreneurship." *The Washington Monthly*. N.p., July 2012. <http://www.washingtonmonthly.com/magazine/julyaugust_2012/features/the_slowmotion_collapse_of_ame038414.php>.
7. Pethokoukis, James. "Crony Capitalism Needs a Kick in the Keister, by James Pethokoukis, National Review." *National Review Online*. N.p., 3 Mar. 2014. <http://www.nationalreview.com/article/372343/crony-capitalism-needs-kick-keister-james-pethokoukis>.
8. Duke, Elizabeth A. "Small Business Credit Availability." *Federalreserve.gov*. Board of Governors of the Federal Reserve System, 14 Apr. 2011. <http://www.federalreserve.gov/newsevents/speech/duke20110414a.htm>.
9. Shane, Scott. "Americans Must Get Back to Starting Businesses." *Bloomberg Business Week*. Bloomberg, 16 Dec. 2011. <http://www.businessweek.com/small-business/americans-must-get-back-to-starting-businesses-12162011.html>.
10. Flash, Cynthia. "Angel Capital Association Takes Action to Avoid Threat to Startup Funding." *Angel Capital Association Takes Action to Avoid Threat to Startup Funding*. The National Edition, 20 May 2014. <http://tech.co/angel-capital-association-takes-action-avoid-threat-startup-funding-potential-sec-rule-changes-eliminate-60-percent-angel-investors-2014-05>.
11. Kaplan, .Steven N., and Josh Lerner. "It Ain't Broke: The Past, Present, and Future of Venture Capital."

Journal of Applied Corporate Finance 22.2 (2010): 1-12. *People.hbs.edu.* Morgan Stanley. <http://www.people.hbs.edu/jlerner/KaplanLerner.JACF.pdf>.

12. Id.

13. Weaver, David, and Jeff Cornwall. "Should Angel Investors Get Tax Credits to Invest in Small Businesses?" *WSJ.* The Wall Street Journal, 19 Mar. 2012. <http://www.wsj.com/news/articles/SB10001424052702304459804577283420497271022>.

14. Clifford, Catherine. "Top Sources of Small-Business Financing in 2012." *Entrepreneur.* N.p., 02 Jan. 2012. <http://www.entrepreneur.com/article/222540>.

15. Id.

16. Duke, Elizabeth A. "Small Business Credit Availability." *Federalreserve.gov.* Board of Governors of the Federal Reserve System, 14 Apr. 2011. <http://www.federalreserve.gov/newsevents/speech/duke20110414a.htm>.

17. Office of the Controller of the Currency. "SBA 7a Guanranteed Loan Program." *Community Developments: Community Affairs Fact Sheet* (n.d.): n. pag. *Occ.gov.* <http://www.occ.gov/topics/community-affairs/publications/fact-sheets/fact-sheet-sba-7a-guaranteed-loan.pdf>.

18. "Rural Business Loans." *Sba.gov.* U.S. Small Business Administration, n.d. Web. <http://www.sba.gov/content/rural-business-loans>.

19. Office of the Controller of the Currency. "SBA 7a Guanranteed Loan Program." *Community Developments: Community Affairs Fact Sheet* (n.d.): n. pag. *Occ.gov.* <http://www.occ.gov/topics/

community-affairs/publications/fact-sheets/fact-sheet-sba-7a-guaranteed-loan.pdf>.

20. Kymn, Christine. "Access to Capital for Women- and Minority-owned Businesses: Revisiting Key Variables." *sba.gov.* Issue Brief Number 3. 29 Jan 2014. <https://www.sba.gov/sites/default/files/Issue%20Brief%203%20Access%20to%20Capital.pdf>

21. Lowry, James H. "Women, Minorities Should Work Together." *Diversity Executive.* November/December 2013. p. 14.

22. Clark, Patrick. "The SBA's Plan to Boost Loans to Minority Entrepreneurs." *Bloomberg.com.* Bloomberg, 10 June 2014. Web. <http://www.bloomberg.com/bw/articles/2014-06-10/the-sbas-plan-to-boost-loans-to-minority-entrepreneurs>.

23. Klein, Karen E. "The SBA Offers Sweeteners to Encourage More Small Loans." *Bloomberg.com.* Bloomberg, 1 Nov. 2013. Web. <http://www.bloomberg.com/bw/articles/2013-11-01/the-sba-offers-sweeteners-to-encourage-more-small-loans>.

24. Clark, Patrick. "The SBA's Plan to Boost Loans to Minority Entrepreneurs." *Bloomberg.com.* Bloomberg, 10 June 2014. <http://www.bloomberg.com/bw/articles/2014-06-10/the-sbas-plan-to-boost-loans-to-minority-entrepreneurs>.

25. Crain, Nicole V., and W. Mark Crain. "The Impact of Regulatory Costs on Small Firms." *SBA Office of Advocacy* (2010): 1-77. *Sba.gov.* SBA Office of Advocacy, Sept. 2010. <https://www.

sba.gov/sites/default/files/The%20Impact%20
of%20Regulatory%20Costs%20on%20Small%20
Firms%20%28Full%29_0.pdf>.

26. Bradford, C. Steven. "Does Size Matter? An
Economic Analysis of Small Business Exemptions
from Regulation." *Southern Economic Journal* 61.4
(1995): 1237-238. *Sec.gov.* <http://www.sec.gov/
info/smallbus/acsec/bradford-doessizematter.
pdf>.

27. "Pesticide Registration Improvement Extension
Act (PRIA 3) of 2012." *EPA.* Environmental
Protection Agency. <http://www.epa.gov/
opp00001/fees/questions/waivers.htm>.

28. "Frequently Asked Questions on Prescription
Drug User Fees (PDUFA)." U.S. Food and
Drug Administration. <http://www.fda.
gov/Drugs/DevelopmentApprovalProcess/
SmallBusinessAssistance/ucm069943.
htm#P227_18912>.

29. Sargeant, Winslow. "The Small Business
Watchdog." United States Small Business
Administration Office of Advocacy, 24 Mar. 2014.
<http://weblog.sba.gov/blog-advo/?p=2580>.

30. "Regulatory Flexibility Act Annual Report of the
Chief Counsel for Advocacy U.S. Small Business
Administration." *Regulatory Flexibility Act Annual
Report of the Chief Counsel for Advocacy U.S. Small
Business Administration.* National Technical
Information Service. <http://archive.sba.gov/
advo/laws/flex/>.

31. Fox, William F. *Understanding Administrative Law.*
New Providence, NJ: LexisNexis, 2012. Print. pp.
178-181.

32. Bergsten, C. Fred. "C. Fred Bergsten - How Best to Boost U.S. Exports." *Washington Post*. The Washington Post, 03 Feb. 2010. <http://www.washingtonpost.com/wp-dyn/content/article/2010/02/02/AR2010020203301.html>.

33. Kirk, Ron. "Advocating Trade to Support American Jobs." *THE PRESIDENT'S TRADE AGENDA* (2012): 1-22. *Ustr.gov*. 1 Mar. 2012. Web. <https://ustr.gov/sites/default/files/Chapter%20I.%20The%20Presidents%202011%20Trade%20Policy%20Agenda.pdf>.

34. Peterson, Kristina, and Michael Crittended. "GOP's Attack on Export-Import Bank Alarms Business Allies." *The Wall Street Journal*. <http://online.wsj.com/articles/gops-attack-on-export-import-bank-alarms-business-allies-1403651509>.

35. Espo, David. "White House, Business Back Export-Import Bank." *The Big Story*. Associated Press, 23 June 2014. <http://bigstory.ap.org/article/white-house-business-back-ex-im-bank>.

36. Carney, Timothy P. "Export-Import Bank Costs Taxpayers $2 Billion a Decade." *AEI*. American Enterprise Institute, 24 May 2014. Web. 10 Feb. 2015. <http://www.aei.org/article/politics-and-public-opinion/export-import-bank-costs-taxpayers-2-billion-a-decade/>.

37. Id.

38. Charlton, Alex. "To save Pa. Jobs, Renew Charter for Ex-Im Bank." *Philly.com*. Interstate General Media, 15 Sept. 2014. Web. 10 Feb. 2015. <http://www.philly.com/philly/opinion/inquirer/20140915_To_save_Pa__jobs__renew_charter_for_Ex-Im_Bank.html>.

39. Espo, David. "White House, Business Back Export-Import Bank." *The Big Story*. Associated Press, 23 June 2014. <http://bigstory.ap.org/article/white-house-business-back-ex-im-bank>.

Chapter 3

40. Northam, Jackie. "As Overseas Costs Rise, More U.S. Companies Are 'Reshoring'" *NPR*. NPR, 27 Jan. 2014. <http://www.npr.org/blogs/parallels/2014/01/22/265080779/as-overseas-costs-rise-more-u-s-companies-are-reshoring>.

41. Coyle, John J., Kusumal Ruamsook, and Evelyn A. Thomchick. "The Real Impact of High Transportation Costs." – *Logistics – CSCMP's Supply Chain Quarterly*. Supply Chain Quarterly, 2014. <http://www.supplychainquarterly.com/topics/Logistics/20140311-the-real-impact-of-high-transportation-costs/>.

42. Marston, Betsy. "Bringing It Home, Keeping It Wild." *High Country News*. 24 Nov. 2011. <https://www.hcn.org/heard-around-the-west/bringing-it-home-keeping-it-wild>.

43. Plumer, Brad. "Is U.S. Manufacturing Making a Comeback - or Is It Just Hype?" *The Washington Post*. 1 May 2013. <http://www.washingtonpost.com/blogs/wonkblog/wp/2013/05/01/is-u-s-manufacturing-set-for-a-comeback-or-is-it-all-hype/>.

44. Mills, Karen. "Small Manufacturers Driving Job Creation, Economic Growth." *Whitehouse.gov*. The White House, 27 Feb. 2012. <http%3A%2F%2Fwww.whitehouse.gov%2Fblog%2F2012%2F02%2F27

%2Fsmall-manufacturers-driving-job-creation-economic-growth>.

45. Sirkin, Harold L. "The Case for Making Small U.S. Manufacturers a Priority." *Bloomberg Business Week*. Bloomberg, 09 Apr. 2013. <http://www.businessweek.com/articles/2013-04-09/the-case-for-making-small-u-dot-s-dot-manufacturers-a-priority>.

46. "Third Planet Windpower." *Third Planet Windpower*. Third Planet Windpower, 2015. <http://www.thirdplanetwind.com/energy/history.aspx>.

47. "Who Invented Solar Panels?" *Who Invented*. 12 Feb. 2011. <http://whoinvented.org/who-invented-solar-panels/>.

48. Sestak, Joe. "Don't Fall for Toomey's Green Energy Scare Tactics." *The Huffington Post*. 15 July 2010. <http://www.huffingtonpost.com/rep-joe-sestak/dont-fall-for-toomeys-gre_b_648072.html>.

49. Lynch, David J., and Robert Schmidt. "Obama's Green Dilemma: Punish China, Imperil U.S. Solar." *Bloomberg*. 18 Aug. 2014. <http://www.bloomberg.com/news/articles/2014-08-18/obama-s-green-dilemma-punish-china-imperil-u-s-solar>.

50. Id.

51. Pollin, Robert, James Heintz, and Heidi Garrett-Peltier. "The Economic Benefits of Investing in Clean Energy." Center for American Progress, June 2009. <http://cdn.americanprogress.org/wp-content/uploads/issues/2009/06/pdf/peri_report.pdf>.

52. Muro, Mark, Jonathan Rothwell, and Devashree Saha. "Sizing the Clean Economy." *Metropolitan Policy Program*. The Brookings Institution. 2011. <http://www.brookings.edu/~/media/series/resources/0713_clean_economy.pdf>.

53. "Shale Gas: Applying Technology to Solve America's Energy Challenges." *Netl.doe.gov*. U.S. Department of Energy and NETL. Mar. 2011. <http://www.netl.doe.gov/file%20library/research/oil-gas/Shale_Gas_March_2011.pdf>.

54. Trembath, Alex, Jesse Jenkins, Ted Nordhaus, and Michael Shellenberger. "Where the Shale Gas Revolution Came From." (2012): *Thebreakthrough.org*. Breakthrough Institute, May 2012. <http://thebreakthrough.org/blog/Where_the_Shale_Gas_Revolution_Came_From.pdf>.

55. Begos, Kevin. "Fracking Developed With Decades Of Government Investment." *The Huffington Post*. 23 Sept. 2012. <http://www.huffingtonpost.com/2012/09/23/fracking-developed-government_n_1907178.html>.

56. Kuuskraa, Vello A., and Hugh D. Guthrie. "Translating Lessons Learned From Unconventional Natural Gas R&D To Geologic Sequestration Technology." *Netl.doe.gov*. NETL. <http://www.netl.doe.gov/publications/proceedings/01/carbon_seq/1a3.pdf>.

57. Id.

58. Tunstall, Thomas. "America's Oil Export Policy Is Stuck in the '70s." *The Wall Street Journal*. 4 Aug. 2014. <http://www.wsj.com/articles/thomas-tunstall-americas-oil-export-policy-is-stuck-in-the-70s-1407195534>.

59. Pirog, Robert. "Oil and Natural Gas Industry Tax Issues in the FY2014 Budget Proposal." *CRS Report for Congress* (2013). Congressional Research Service. 30 Oct. 2013. <http://assets.opencrs.com/rpts/R42374_20131030.pdf>.

60. "Business Energy Investment Tax Credit (ITC)." *Dsireusa.org*. NC State University, 13 Mar. 2014. <http://www.dsireusa.org/incentives/incentive.cfm?Incentive_Code=US02F>.

61. Donoghue, Lauren. "House Approves Bill to Make R&D Tax Credit Permanent." *Lexology.com*. King & Spalding LLP. 3 June 2014. <https://www.lexology.com/library/detail.aspx?g=5d9f2120-751e-427a-a396-699a53abcc31>.

62. "R&D, Patents Are Key Manufacturing Drivers Chief Economist Mark Doms Tells National Association for Business Economics 2012 Conference." *Commerce.gov*. Department of Commerce, 31 May 2012. <http://www.commerce.gov/blog/2012/05/31/rd-patents-are-key-manufacturing-drivers-chief-economist-mark-doms-tells-national-as>.

63. "Facts & Statistics." *Business Incentive Solutions*. 2013. <http://www.businessincentivesolutions.com/facts_and_statistics.html>.

64. "R&D, Patents Are Key Manufacturing Drivers Chief Economist Mark Doms Tells National Association for Business Economics 2012 Conference." *Commerce.gov*. Department of Commerce. 31 May 2012. <http://www.commerce.gov/blog/2012/05/31/rd-patents-are-key-manufacturing-drivers-chief-economist-mark-doms-tells-national-as>.

65. Sestak, Joe. "Go With What Works." *The Huffington Post*. 8 Sept. 2011. <http://www.huffingtonpost.com/rep-joe-sestak/go-with-what-works_b_954561.html>.

66. Kuznicki, Kathleen. "How Long Does It Take to Get a Patent?" *Exitpromise.com*. 3 Apr. 2014. <http://exitpromise.com/patent-approval-process>.

67. Schmid, John, and Ben Poston. "Patent Office Overseer Quits Agency." *Jsonline.com*. Journal Sentinel, 11 Sept. 2009. <http://www.jsonline.com/watchdog/watchdogreports/58750302.html>.

68. Brachmann, Steve. "PTO Deputy Michelle Lee Says the Patent System Needs Change." *IPWatchdog.com*. 1 July 2014. <http://www.ipwatchdog.com/2014/07/01/pto-deputy-michelle-lee-says-the-patent-system-needs-change/id=50250/>.

69. Draper, Heather. "Colorado Leaders Celebrate Opening of New Patent Office in Denver (Slideshow)." *Denver Business Journal*. 30 June 2014. <http://www.bizjournals.com/denver/blog/finance_etc/2014/06/colorado-leaders-celebrate-opening-of-new-patent.html?page=all>.

70. Kuznicki, Kathleen. "How Long Does It Take to Get a Patent?" *Exitpromise.com*. 3 Apr. 2014. <http://exitpromise.com/patent-approval-process>.

71. "China Effects of Intellectual Property Infringement and Indigenous Innovation Policies on the U.S. Economy: Investigation No. 332-519." U.S. International Trade Commission. May 2011. <http://www.usitc.gov/publications/332/pub4226.pdf>.

Chapter 4

72. "2013 Report Card for America's Infrastructure." The American Society of Civil Engineers, Mar. 2013. <http://www.infrastructurereportcard. org/a/documents/2013-Report-Card.pdf>.
73. Davis, Stephen L., and David Goldberg. "The Fix We're In For: The State of Our Nation's Bridges 2013." Transportation for America, 19 June 2013. <http://t4america.org/docs/bridgereport2013/2 013BridgeReport.pdf>.
74. Hartgen, David T., and M. Gregory Fields. "21st Annual Report on the Performance of State Highway Systems (1984-2012)." Reason.org, Sept. 2014. <http://reason.org/files/21st_annual_ highway_report.pdf>.
75. "Policy Statement 521 - Rail Infrastructure Investment." The American Society of Civil Engineers, 2013. <http://www.asce.org/ issues-and-advocacy/public-policy/policy-statement-521—rail-infrastructure-investment/>.
76. "2013 Report Card for America's Infrastructure." The American Society of Civil Engineers, Mar. 2013. <http://www.infrastructurereportcard. org/a/documents/2013-Report-Card.pdf>.
77. Id.
78. Crawford, Susan. "It's Time to Fix the Pitifully Slow, Expensive Internet Access in the U.S." *Wired. com.* Conde Nast Digital. 13 Dec. 2012. <http:// www.wired.com/2012/12/hey-dont-forget-about-internet-access-in-the-u-s/>.
79. Mahapatra, Lisa. "24 Countries With Better Infrastructure Than America." *Business Insider.* 10 Mar. 2013. <http://www.businessinsider.

com/countries-with-better-infrastructure-2013-3?op=1>.
80. "Failure to Act Economic Studies." *ASCE.com.* The American Society of Civil Engineers, 15 Jan. 2013. <http://www.asce.org/failure_to_act_economic_studies/>.
81. Casey, Robert P. "Casey: Federal Highway Projects Across PA, Nation Could Grind to Halt In Weeks Without Action by Congress." *www.casey.senate.gov.* 26 June 2014. <http://www.casey.senate.gov/newsroom/releases/casey-federal-highway-projects-across-pa-nation-could-grind-to-halt-in-weeks-without-action-by-congress>.
82. "An Economic Analysis of Infrastructure Investment." *Whitehouse.gov.* The Department of the Treasury with the Council of Economic Advisers, 11 Oct. 2010. <http://www.whitehouse.gov/sites/default/files/infrastructure_investment_report.pdf>.
83. Snyder, Tanya. "Senators Murphy (D) and Corker (R) Propose 12-Cent Gas Tax Increase." *Streetsblog USA.*18 June 2014. <http://usa.streetsblog.org/2014/06/18/sens-chris-murphy-d-and-bob-corker-r-propose-12-cent-gas-tax-increase/>.
84. Geddes, Rick, and Brad Wassink. "Bring Highway Funding Up to Speed." The Wall Street Journal, 16 June 2014. <http://www.wsj.com/articles/rick-geddes-and-brad-wassink-bring-highway-funding-up-to-speed-1402961161>.
85. Laing, Keith. "Consumer Group: Drivers Buying More Fuel Efficient Cars." *TheHill.* 23 June 2014. <http://thehill.com/policy/

transportation/210272-consumer-group-drivers-buying-more-fuel-efficient-cars>.

86. LoGiurato, Brett. "Two Senators Have A Very Simple And Very Unpopular Idea For Saving The Highway Trust Fund." *Business Insider*. 18 June 2014. <http://www.businessinsider.com/highway-trust-fund-solution-gas-tax-hike-corker-murphy-2014-6#ixzz35C3BFD3b>.

87. Id.

88. Harrison, David. "Conservatives See Highway Trust Fund Fight as Road to State Control of Transportation Spending." *RollCall.com*. 23 June 2014. <http://www.rollcall.com/news/conservatives_see_highway_trust_fund_fight_as_road_to_state_control_of-234140-1.html?pg=3&dczone=policy>.

89. "Using Public-Private Partnerships to Carry Out Highway Projects." *Www.cbo.gov*. Congress of the United States Congressional Budget Office, Jan. 2012. <http://www.cbo.gov/sites/default/files/cbofiles/attachments/01-09-PublicPrivatePartnerships.pdf>.

90. Usdan, Jordan, and Kevin Almasy. "FCC Chairman Announces Jobs-Focused Digital Literacy Partnership Between Connect2Compete and the 2,800 American Job Centers." *Broadband.gov*. Federal Communications Commission, 23 July 2012. <http://blog.broadband.gov/?entryId=1718810>.

91. Litan, Robert E., and Hal J. Singer. *The Need for Speed: A New Framework for Telecommunications Policy for the 21st Century*. 2013. 61-62.

92. "Comcast to Buy Time Warner Cable for $45 Billion." *Crain's Chicago Business*. N.p., 13 Feb.

2014. <http://www.chicagobusiness.com/ article/20140213/NEWS07/140219883/comcast-to-buy-time-warner-cable-for-45-billion#>.

93. Verizon v. FCC & USA, No. 11-1355 (D.C. Cir.). Brief for Appellee/Respondents .

94. "Comcast to Buy Time Warner Cable for $45 Billion." *Crain's Chicago Business*. N.p., 13 Feb. 2014. <http://www.chicagobusiness.com/ article/20140213/NEWS07/140219883/comcast-to-buy-time-warner-cable-for-45-billion#>.

95. Fung, Brian. "Twenty States Bar Cities from Building Their Own Internet. Netflix Wants the FCC to Change That." The Washington Post, 3 Sept. 2014. <http://www.washingtonpost.com/blogs/ the-switch/wp/2014/09/03/twenty-states-bar-cities-from-building-their-own-internet-netflix-wants-the-fcc-to-change-that/>.

96. Id.

97. See S.1193 - Data Security and Breach Notification Act of 2013.

98. Sestak, Joe. "Rural Job Retention, Growth Depend on Net Access."*Times Leader*. 14 July 2013. <http://timesleader.com/news/ othercommentary/669916/Rural-job-retention-growth-depend-on-Net-access>.

99. Id.

Chapter 5

100. Thomas, Kenneth. "Basics: Real Wages Remain Below Their Peak for 39th Straight Year." Middle Class Political Economist. 12 Mar. 2012. <http://www.middleclasspoliticaleconomist.

com/2012/03/basics-real-wages-remain-below-their.html>.

101. "Characteristics of Minimum Wage Workers: 2012." (2013): 1-14. Bureau of Labor Statistics U.S. Department of Labor, 26 Feb. 2013. <http://www. bls.gov/cps/minwage2012.pdf>.

102. Covert, Bryce. "Walmart CEO Claims 'Vast Majority' Of Workers Make More Than Minimum Wage." ThinkProgress RSS. 26 Aug. 2013. <http:// thinkprogress.org/economy/2013/08/26/2525871/ walmart-minimum-wage/>.

103. "Making Change at Walmart » Walmart and Workers." Making Change at Walmart RSS. <http://makingchangeatwalmart.org/walmart-and-workers/#_ftn3>.

104. "Tables 1 - 10." U.S. Bureau of Labor Statistics. 26 Feb. 2013. <http://www.bls.gov/cps/ minwage2012tbls.htm>.

105. Jones, Janelle, and John Schmitt. "The Minimum Wage Is Not What It Used To Be | CEPR Blog." Center for Economic and Policy Research. 17 July 2013. <http://www.cepr.net/index.php/blogs/ cepr-blog/the-minimum-wage-is-not-what-it-used-to-be>.

106. "Minimum Wage Mythbusters." U.S. Department of Labor. <http://www.dol.gov/minwage/ mythbuster.htm>.

107. Blinder, Alan S. "'Pikettymania' and Inequality in the U.S." *The Wall Street Journal*. <http://www. wsj.com/articles/alan-blinder-pikettymania-and-inequality-in-the-u-s-1403477052>.

108. Blinder, Alan S. "'Pikettymania' and Inequality in the U.S." *The Wall Street Journal*. 22 June 2014. <http://

www.wsj.com/articles/alan-blinder-pikettymania-and-inequality-in-the-u-s-1403477052>.

109. Blinder, Alan S. "'Pikettymania' and Inequality in the U.S." *The Wall Street Journal*. 22 June 2014. <http://www.wsj.com/articles/alan-blinder-pikettymania-and-inequality-in-the-u-s-1403477052>.

110. Blinder, Alan S. "'Pikettymania' and Inequality in the U.S." *The Wall Street Journal*. 22 June 2014. <http://www.wsj.com/articles/alan-blinder-pikettymania-and-inequality-in-the-u-s-1403477052>.

111. Politi, James. "US Jobs: Slim Pickings - FT.com." Financial Times. 20 July 2014. <http://www.ft.com/cms/s/2/3676ad9e-0de1-11e4-b149-00144feabdc0.html#axzz3RPGAp27D>.

112. "Employment Characteristics of Families Summary." U.S. Bureau of Labor Statistics. U.S. Bureau of Labor Statistics, 25 Apr. 2014. <http://www.bls.gov/news.release/famee.nr0.htm>.

113. "Working Family Values Factoids." PBS. <http://www.pbs.org/livelyhood/workingfamily/familytrends.html>.

114. Politi, James. "US Jobs: Slim Pickings - FT.com." Financial Times. 20 July 2014. <http://www.ft.com/cms/s/2/3676ad9e-0de1-11e4-b149-00144feabdc0.html#axzz3RPGAp27D>.

115. "Report of the Interdepartmental Committee Concerning the Review of the Criteria to Determine the Minimum Wage – Summary and Recommendations." 12 Mar. 2002. <https://www.travail.gouv.qc.ca/fileadmin/fichiers/

Documents/normes_travail/salaire_minimum/summary2.pdf>.

116. Solman, Paul. "The Man and the Thinking Behind the Minimum Wage Hike." PBS. 14 Feb. 2013. <http://www.pbs.org/newshour/making-sense/the-man-behind-the-minimum-wag/>.

117. "Average Hourly Pay and Pay Inequality, 1948–2011 (2011 Dollars)." *State of Working America.* Economic Policy Institute. <http://www.stateofworkingamerica.org/chart/swa-wages-table-4-2-average-hourly-pay-inequality/>.

118. Card, David E. Minimum Wages and Employment: A Case Study of the Fast-food Industry in New Jersey and Pennsylvania. Princeton, NJ: Industrial Relations Section, Dept of Economics, Princeton U, 1994. University of Huston, 2001. <http://www.uh.edu/~adkugler/Card%26Krueger.pdf>.

119. Michael Reich, Ken Jacobs, and Annette Bernhardt. (2014). "Local Minimum Wage Laws: Impacts on Workers, Families and Businesses". IRLE Working Paper No. 104-14. <http://irle.berkeley.edu/workingpapers/104-14.pdf>.

120. Democratic Staff of the U.S. House Committee on Education and the Workforce. "The Low-Wage Drag on Our Economy: Wal-Mart's Low Wages and Their Effect on Taxpayers and Economic Growth."*Democrats - U.S. House Committee on Education and the Workforce.* May 2013. <http://democrats.edworkforce.house.gov/sites/democrats.edworkforce.house.gov/files/documents/WalMartReport-May2013.pdf>.

121. Gandel, Stephen. "Why Wal-Mart Can Afford to Give Its Workers a 50% raise." *Fortune.* 12 Nov.

2013. <http://fortune.com/2013/11/12/why-wal-mart-can-afford-to-give-its-workers-a-50-raise/>.

122. Ritholtz, Barry. "How McDonald's and Wal-Mart Became Welfare Queens." Bloomberg. 13 Nov. 2013. <http://www.bloombergview.com/articles/2013-11-13/how-mcdonald-s-and-wal-mart-became-welfare-queens>.

123. Rugaber, Christopher. "US States with Higher Minimum Wages Gain More Jobs." The Big Story. The Associated Press, 19 July 2014. <http://bigstory.ap.org/article/us-states-higher-minimum-wages-gain-more-jobs>.

124. Belsie, Laurent. "Job Loss in the Great Recession." The Digest. <http://www.nber.org/digest/sep11/w17040.html>.

125. Canon, Maria, Marianna Kudlyak, and Marisa Reed. "Is Involuntary Part-time Employment Different after the Great Recession?" Federal Reserve Bank of St. Louis, July 2014. <https://www.stlouisfed.org/Publications/Regional-Economist/July-2014/Is-Involuntary-Parttime-Employment-Different-after-the-Great-Recession>.

126. Samuelson, Robert. "A Part-timer Boom, or Blip?" Washington Post. *The Washington Post*. 16 July 2014. <http://www.washingtonpost.com/opinions/robert-samuelson-a-part-timer-boom-or-blip/2014/07/16/9fb8527a-0cf7-11e4-b8e5-d0de80767fc2_story.html>.

127. Smith, Rebecca, and Claire Mckenna. "Temped Out: How the Domestic Outsourcing of Blue-Collar Jobs Harms America's Workers." National Employment Law Project. 10 July 2014. <http://nelp.3cdn.net/ad4435f58bca300039_a1em6bvsb.pdf>.

128. Klein, Ezra. "Obamacare's Employer Mandate Shouldn't Be Delayed. It Should Be Repealed." *The Washington Post.* 2 July 2014. <http://www.washingtonpost.com/blogs/wonkblog/wp/2013/07/02/obamacares-employer-mandate-shouldnt-be-delayed-it-should-be-repealed/>.

129. "The Impact of Health Reform on the Individual Insurance Market." Deloitte Issue Brief. *Deloitte.* 2011. <http://www2.deloitte.com/content/dam/Deloitte/us/Documents/Health%20Reform%20Issues%20Briefs/us_chs_HealthReformAndThe IndividualInsuranceMarket_IssueBrief_101011.pdf>.

130. Millman, Jason. "Large Employers Are Getting Their Premiums under Control, but You're Probably Paying More." *The Washington Post.* 3 Apr. 2014. <http://www.washingtonpost.com/blogs/wonkblog/wp/2014/04/03/large-employers-are-getting-their-premiums-under-control-but-youre-probably-paying-more/>.

131. Ehley, Brianna. "Obamacare Sticker Shock Found in Deductibles, Not Premiums." *The Fiscal Times.* 3 Feb. 2014. <http://www.thefiscaltimes.com/Articles/2014/02/03/Obamacare-Sticker-Shock-Found-Deductibles-Not-Premiums>.

132. Id.

133. Rau, Jordan. "The 10 Least Expensive Health Insurance Markets In The U.S." Kaiser Health News. 13 Feb. 2014. <http://kaiserhealthnews.org/news/10-least-expensive-health-insurance-markets-in-us/>.

134. The Affordable Care Act and Employer-Sponsored Insurance for Working Americans." Academy Health. 2011. <http://www.academyhealth.org/

files/nhpc/2011/AH_2011AffordableCareReport FINAL3.pdf>.

135. Worstall, Tim. "Apple's 9.8% Tax Rate." *Forbes.* Forbes Magazine, 18 Apr. 2012. <http://www. forbes.com/sites/timworstall/2012/04/18/ apples-9-8-tax-rate-entirely-mind-gargling-nonsense/>.

136. "Google 2.4% Rate Shows How $60 Billion Is Lost to Tax Loopholes." *Bloomberg News.* 21 Oct. 2010. <http://www.bloomberg.com/news/ articles/2010-10-21/google-2-4-rate-shows-how-60-billion-u-s-revenue-lost-to-tax-loopholes>.

137. "Treasury Fact Sheet: The New Rules on Tax Inversions." *The Wall Street Journal.* 22 Sept. 2014. <http://blogs.wsj.com/washwire/2014/09/22/ treasury-fact-sheet-the-new-rules-on-tax-inversions/>.

138. Drawbaugh, Kevin. "More U.S. Companies Doing Deals to Avoid U.S. Taxes: Congress Study." *Reuters.* 07 July 2014. <http://www.reuters. com/article/2014/07/07/us-usa-tax-inversion-idUSKBN0FC29C20140707>.

139. Montgomery, Lori. "U.S. Policymakers Gird for Rash of Corporate Expatriations." *The Washington Post.* 6 Aug. 2014. <http://www.washingtonpost.com/ business/economy/us-policymakers-gird-for-rash-of-corporate-expatriations/2014/08/05/4898ca5e-18d9-11e4-9349-84d4a85be981_story.html>.

140. Sorkin, Andrew Ross. "At Walgreen, Renouncing Corporate Citizenship." *The New York Times.* 30 June 2014. <http://dealbook.nytimes.com/2014/06/30/ renouncing-corporate-citizenship/>.

141. "Michael McCaul Says U.S. Corporate Tax Rate Is World's Highest at 35 Percent." PolitiFact. 1 Nov. 2012. <http://www.politifact.com/texas/statements/2012/nov/01/michael-mccaul/michael-mccaul-says-us-corporate-tax-rate-worlds-h/>.

142. Ritholtz, Barry. "The U.S. Corporate Tax Dodge." *Bloomberg*. 9 Jan. 2014. <http://www.bloombergview.com/articles/2014-07-09/the-u-s-corporate-tax-dodge>.

143. "Corporate Income Tax: Effective Tax Rates Can Differ Significantly from the Statutory Rate." United States Government Accountability Office. May 2013. <http://gao.gov/assets/660/654957.pdf>.

144. Winograd, David. "Some Small Businesses Pay Tax Rates More Than Double Those Of Large Corporations:Study." *The Huffington Post.* 8 Aug. 2013. <http://www.huffingtonpost.com/2013/08/08/small-business-taxes_n_3727270.html>.

145. Jacobson, Louis. "Bernie Sanders Says Tax Share Paid by Corporations Has Fallen from 33% to 9% since 1952." PolitiFact. 28 Aug. 2014. <http://www.politifact.com/truth-o-meter/statements/2014/aug/28/bernie-s/bernie-sanders-says-tax-share-paid-corporations-ha/>.

146. "Where Do Federal Tax Revenues Come From?" Center on Budget and Policy Priorities. 31 Mar. 2014. <http://www.cbpp.org/cms/?fa=view&id=3822>.

147. Drawbaugh, Kevin, and Patrick Temple-West. "Untaxed U.S. Corporate Profits Held Overseas Top $2.1 Trillion: Study." *Reuters*. 08 Apr. 2014. <http://www.reuters.com/article/2014/04/09/us-usa-tax-offshore-idUSBREA3729V20140409>.

148. Tsang, Derek. "Does the U.S. Have the Highest Corporate Tax Rate in the Free World?" PolitiFact. 9 Sept. 2014. <http://www.politifact.com/punditfact/statements/2014/sep/09/eric-bolling/does-us-have-highest-corporate-tax-rate-free-world/>.

Chapter 6

149. Sestak, Joe. "Stop Dividing Americans: Both the 47 Percent and the 1 Percent Seek a Better Country." *Pittsburgh Post-Gazette.* 26 Mar. 2013. <http://www.post-gazette.com/opinion/Op-Ed/2013/03/26/Stop-dividing-Americans-Both-the-47-percent-and-the-1-percent-seek-a-better-country/stories/201303260132>.

150. Needleman, Sarah. "Skills Shortage Means Many Jobs Go Unfilled." The Wall Street Journal, 9 July 2014. <http://www.wsj.com/articles/small-business-owners-work-to-fill-job-openings-1404940118>.

151. Martin, John P. "Activation and Active Labour Market Policies in OECD Countries: Stylized Facts and Evidence on Their Effectiveness." IZA Policy Paper Series, June 2014. Web. <http://ftp.iza.org/pp84.pdf>.

152. Weber, Lauren. "Just Whose Job Is It to Train Workers?" The Wall Street Journal, 16 June 2014. <http://www.wsj.com/articles/just-whose-job-is-it-to-train-workers-1405554382>.

153. Zumbrun, Josh. "Blame Employers, Not Workers, for Any Skills Gap, Economist Says." The Wall Street Journal, 18 Aug. 2014. <http://blogs.wsj.com/economics/2014/08/18/blame-employers-not-workers-for-any-skills-gap-economist-says/>.

154. "The Workforce Innovation and Opportunity Act: Investing in America's Workforce" *Edworkforce.house. gov.* <http://edworkforce.house.gov/uploadedfiles/ workforce_innovation_and_opportunity_act_-_one_ pager.pdf>.
155. Jacoby, Tamar. "This Way Up: Mobility in America." The Wall Street Journal, 22 July 2014. <http://www.wsj.com/articles/this-way-up-mobility-in-america-1405710779>.
156. Garver, Rob. "Self-Congratulation in Congress Does Little for the Jobless." *The Fiscal Times.* 14 July 2014. <http://www.thefiscaltimes.com/ Columns/2014/07/14/Self-Congratulation-Congress-Does-Little-Jobless>.
157. Garver, Rob. "Time to Fix Failed $18 Billion Job Training Programs." *The Fiscal Times.* 3 Feb. 2014. <http://www.thefiscaltimes.com/ Articles/2014/02/03/Time-Fix-Failed-18-Billion-Job-Training-Programs>.
158. "The Workforce Innovation and Opportunity Act: Investing in America's Workforce" *Edworkforce.house. gov.* <http://edworkforce.house.gov/uploadedfiles/ workforce_innovation_and_opportunity_act_-_one_ pager.pdf>.
159. Schoof, Renee. "Workforce Training to Get an Upgrade under Bill Heading for Obama's Signature." McClatchy, 11 July 2014. <http:// www.mcclatchydc.com/2014/07/11/233108/ workforce-training-to-get-an-upgrade.html>.
160. Williams, Timothy. "Seeking New Start, Finding Steep Cost." The New York Times, 17 Aug. 2014. <http://www.nytimes.com/2014/08/18/us/

workforce-investment-act-leaves-many-jobless-and-in-debt.html>.

161. Williams, Timothy. "Seeking New Start, Finding Steep Cost." The New York Times, 17 Aug. 2014. <http://www.nytimes.com/2014/08/18/us/workforce-investment-act-leaves-many-jobless-and-in-debt.html>.

162. Gardner, T. M. Human resource alliances: defining the construct and exploring the antecedents. *The International Journal of Human Resource Management*, 16(6), 1049-1066. 2005. <https://www.huntsman.usu.edu/files/uploads/Publications/Human%20Resource%20Alliances.pdf>.

163. Smith, Tara Carter and Christopher T. King. (2011). Exploratory Return-on-Investment Analysis of Local Workforce Investments, Austin: Ray Marshall Center for the Study of Human Resources, Lyndon B. Johnson School of Public Affairs, University of Texas at Austin. August 2011. <http://www.utexas.edu/research/cshr/pubs/pdf/Capital_IDEA_ROI_Final_Aug_23_2011.pdf>.

164. Quinton, Sophie. "The Job Training Program That Actually Works." The National Journal, 12 June 2014. <http://www.nationaljournal.com/next-economy/america-360/the-job-training-program-that-actually-works-20140612>.

165. Rothschild, Steve. "Human Capital Performance Bonds." *Federal Reserve Bank of San Francisco.* Community Development Investment Review, Apr. 2013. Web. <http://www.frbsf.org/community-development/files/human-capital-performance-bonds.pdf>.

166. Id.

Chapter 7

167. Farley, Robert. "ACA Impact on Per Capita Cost of Health Care." *FactCheck.org.* 14 Feb. 2014. <http://www.factcheck.org/2014/02/aca-impact-on-per-capita-cost-of-health-care/>; See also National Health Spending In 2013: Growth Slows, Remains in Step with the Overall Economy. Health Affairs. <http://content.healthaffairs.org/content/early/2014/11/25/hlthaff.2014.1107.full.pdf+html>.

168. Farley, Robert. "ACA Impact on Per Capita Cost of Health Care." *FactCheck.org.* 14 Feb. 2014. <http://www.factcheck.org/2014/02/aca-impact-on-per-capita-cost-of-health-care/>; see also Armour, Stephanie. "Health Spending Grew 3.6% in 2013, Projections Show." The Wall Street Journal, 3 Sept. 2014. <http://www.wsj.com/articles/health-spending-grew-3-6-in-2013-projections-show-1409774427>.

169. *Health Insurance Premiums: Comparing ACA Exchange Rates to the Employer-based Market* (n.d.): n. pag. *PricewaterhouseCoopers.* 2014. Web. <http://www.pwc.com/us/en/health-industries/health-research-institute/assets/pwc-hri-health-insurance-premium.pdf>.

170. "Health Plan Choice and Premiums in the 2015 Health Insurance Marketplace." *aspe.hhs.gov.* ASPE Office of Health Policy, 8 Jan. 2015. <http://aspe.hhs.gov/health/reports/2015/premiumreport/healthpremium2015.pdf>.

171. Millman, Jason. "Lower Premiums (yes, really) Drive down Obamacare's Expected Costs, CBO Says." The Washington Post, 14 Apr. 2014. <http://

www.washingtonpost.com/blogs/wonkblog/
wp/2014/04/14/lower-premiums-yes-really-
drive-down-obamacares-expected-costs-cbo-
says/>.

172. Wilde Mathews, Anna. "California Sees Health-Law Premiums Rising 4.2% in 2015." The Wall Street Journal, 31 July 2014. <http://www.wsj.com/articles/california-sees-health-law-premiums-rising-4-2-in-2015-1406841981>.

173. Id.

174. Cox, Cynthia, Larry Levitt, Gary Claxton, and Rosa Ma. "Analysis of 2015 Premium Changes in the Affordable Care Act's Health Insurance Marketplaces." Kaiser Family Foundation, Jan. 2015. <http://kff.org/health-reform/issue-brief/analysis-of-2015-premium-changes-in-the-affordable-care-acts-health-insurance-marketplaces/>.

175. Millman, Jason. "More Insurers Line up to Sell Obamacare Plans in 2015, HHS Says." The Washington Post, 23 Sept. 2014. <http://www.washingtonpost.com/blogs/wonkblog/wp/2014/09/23/more-insurers-line-up-to-sell-obamacare-plans-in-2015-hhs-says/>.

176. Gunja, Munira Z., and Emily R. Gee. "Health Insurance Issuer Participation and New Entrants in the Health Insurance Marketplace in 2015." *Aspe.hhs.gov*. ASPE Office of Health Policy, 23 Sept. 2014. <http://aspe.hhs.gov/health/reports/2014/NewEntrants/ib_NewEntrants.pdf>.

177. Gabel, Jon. "The Small Business Health Options Program." *Smallbusiness.house.gov*. Testimony before the U.S. House Committee on

Small Business, Subcommittee on Health and Technology, 18 Sept. 2014. <http://smallbusiness. house.gov/uploadedfiles/9-18-2014_gabel_ revised_testimony.pdf>.

178. Al-Faruque, Ferdous. "HHS: O-Care Saved Billions in Drug Costs." TheHill, 29 July 2014. <http:// thehill.com/policy/healthcare/213676-hhs-o- care-saved-billions-in-drug-costs>.

179. Humer, Caroline. "U.S. Health Insurers to Pay $330 Million in Premium Rebates." *Reuters.* 24 July 2014. <http://www.reuters.com/article/2014/07/24/ us-usa-healthcare-insurance-idUSKBN0FT0 9F20140724>.

180. Id.

181. Id.

182. "A Summary of the 2014 Annual Reports." *Trustees Report Summary.* Social Security Administration. <http://www.ssa.gov/oact/trsum/>.

183. Paletta, Damian. "Medicare, Social Security Disability Fund Headed in Different Directions." The Wall Street Journal. 28 July 2014. <http:// www.wsj.com/articles/medicare-social-security- headed-in-different-directions-1406564712>.

184. Id.

185. Wayne, Alexander. "Obamacare Dividends Pile Up for Hospitals as Patients Pay." *Bloomberg,* 30 July 2014. <http://www.bloomberg.com/news/ articles/2014-07-30/obamacare-dividends-pile- up-for-hospitals-as-patients-pay>.

186. "Medicare's Basic Monthly Premium Unchanged in 2015." *The Boston Globe.* 10 Oct. 2014. Web. 15 Feb. 2015. <http://www. bostonglobe.com/news/nation/2014/10/10/

medicare-basic-monthly-premium-unchanged/
TvNLAAumGrrY5zvOPWFsFK/story.html>.

187. Rovner, Julie. "Good News For Boomers: Medicare's Hospital Trust Fund Appears Flush Until 2030." *Kaiser Health News*. 28 July 2014. <http://kaiserhealthnews.org/news/medicare-trustees-say-fund-will-last-until-2030/>.

188. Brennan, Niall. "Findings from Recent CMS Research on Medicare." Centers for Medicare and Medicaid Services. <http://www.academyhealth.org/files/2014/monday/brennan.pdf>.

189. "Interim Update on 2013 Annual Hospital-Acquired Condition Rate and Estimates of Cost Savings and Deaths Averted From 2010 to 2013." *Ahrq.gov*. Agency for Health Research and Quality. <http://www.ahrq.gov/professionals/quality-patient-safety/pfp/interimhacrate2013.pdf>.

190. Millman, Jason. "Most Obamacare Exchange Enrollees Were Previously Uninsured, Survey Finds." *The Washington Post*. 19 June 2014. <http://www.washingtonpost.com/blogs/wonkblog/wp/2014/06/19/most-obamacare-exchange-enrollees-were-previously-uninsured-survey-finds/>.

191. "Hidden Costs, Value Lost: Uninsurance in America." The Institute of Medicine. June 2003. <http://www.iom.edu/~/media/Files/Report%20Files/2003/Hidden-Costs-Value-Lost-Uninsurance-in-America/Uninsured5FINAL.pdf>.

192. Wheaton, Sarah. "More Signs That Health Coverage Is Growing under Obamacare." *POLITICO*. 10 July 2014. <http://www.politico.

com/story/2014/07/health-coverage-growing-under-obamacare-108785.html>.

193. Haberkorn, Jennifer. "7.3 Million in Obamacare Plans, Beats CBO Forecast." *POLITICO*. 18 Sept. 2014. <http://www.politico.com/story/2014/09/obamacare-enrollment-numbers-111097.html>.

194. Wheaton, Sarah. "More Signs That Health Coverage Is Growing under Obamacare." *POLITICO*. 10 July 2014. <http://www.politico.com/story/2014/07/health-coverage-growing-under-obamacare-108785.html>.

195. Lauter, David. "Most Obamacare Enrollees Happy with New Coverage, Data Show." *The Los Angeles Times*. 10 July 2014. Web. 15 Feb. 2015. <http://www.latimes.com/nation/la-na-obamacare-coverage-20140710-story.html>.

196. Wolfson, Elijah. "US Patients Again Look to Canada in Quest for Affordable Medication" *Al Jazeera America*. 7 Nov. 2013.<http://america.aljazeera.com/articles/2013/11/7/is-canada-the-answertohighpriceofmedsinus.html>.

197. Id.

198. "International Federation of Health Plans 2012 Comparative Price Report." International Federation of Health Plans. <http://hushp.harvard.edu/sites/default/files/downloadable_files/IFHP%202012%20Comparative%20Price%20Report.pdf>.

199. "Klobuchar, McCain Introduce Bipartisan Legislation to Reduce Prescription Drug Costs." *Www.klobuchar.senate.gov*. U.S. Senator Amy Klobuchar. 8 July 2014. <http://www.klobuchar.

senate.gov/public/news-releases?ID=ba3ff610-4751-4521-8fa9-f3c53c30f8ef>.

200. "Persuading the Prescribers: Pharmaceutical Industry Marketing and Its Influence on Physicians and Patients." PEW Charitable Trusts. 11 Nov. 2013. <http://www.pewtrusts.org/en/research-and-analysis/fact-sheets/2013/11/11/persuading-the-prescribers-pharmaceutical-industry-marketing-and-its-influence-on-physicians-and-patients>.

201. $27 billion divided by $4 million (the cost of a 30 second spot) equals 6,750.

202. Lachman, Samantha. "McCain, Klobuchar Team Up On Bill Allowing Prescription Drug Imports From Canada." *The Huffington Post.* 9 July 2014. <http://www.huffingtonpost.com/2014/07/09/john-mccain-amy-klobuchar_n_5568415.html>.

203. "Require Manufacturers to Pay a Minimum Rebate on Drugs Covered Under Part D of Medicare for Low-Income Beneficiaries." *Congressional Budget Office.* 20 Nov. 2013. <http://www.cbo.gov/budget-options/2013/44899>.

204. "Price Negotiation for the Medicare Drug Program: It Is Time to Lower Costs for Seniors." The National Committee to Preserve Social Security and Medicare. Oct. 2009. <http://www.ncpssm.org/pdf/price_negotiation_part_d.pdf>.

205. Hamilton, Martha. "Allow Medicare to Negotiate for Cheaper Drug Prices." *PolitiFact.* 25 Apr. 2012. <http://www.politifact.com/truth-o-meter/promises/obameter/promise/73/allow-medicare-to-negotiate-for-cheaper-drug-price/>.

206. Hamburger, Tom. "White House Deal with Drug Firms Draws Flak." *The Los Angeles Times*. 14 Aug. 2009. <http://www.latimes.com/nation/la-na-health-pharma14-2009aug14-story.html>.
207. Gold, Jenny. "ACOs Saving Some Money, But Medicare Is Short On Details." *Kaiser Health News*. 31 Jan. 2014. <http://kaiserhealthnews.org/news/acos-saving-some-money-but-medicare-is-short-on-details/>.
208. Muhlestein, David. "Continued Growth Of Public And Private Accountable Care Organizations." *Health Affairs*. 19 Feb. 2013. <http://healthaffairs.org/blog/2013/02/19/continued-growth-of-public-and-private-accountable-care-organizations/>.
209. "Accountable Care Organizations Now Serve 14% of Americans." Oliver Wyman, 19 Feb. 2013. <http://www.oliverwyman.com/content/dam/oliver-wyman/global/en/files/archive/2012/ACO_press_release%282%29.pdf>.
210. "Statement of Antitrust Enforcement Policy Regarding Accountable Care Organizations Participating in the Medicare Shared Savings Program." *Justice.gov*. Federal Trade Commission / Department of Justice, 2011. <http://www.justice.gov/atr/public/health_care/276458.pdf>.
211. "Higher Use of Advanced Imaging Services by Providers Who Self-Refer Costing Medicare Millions." Government Accountability Office, Sept. 2012. <http://www.gao.gov/assets/650/648989.pdf>.
212. Able, Benjamin H. "The Stark Physician Self-Referral Law and Accountable Care Organizations:

Collision Course or Opportunity to Reconcile Federal Anti-Abuse and Cost-Saving Legislation?" Cleveland-Marshall College of Law Library, 2013. <http://engagedscholarship.csuohio.edu/cgi/viewcontent.cgi?article=1343&context=jlh>.

213. "Pay for Delay." Federal Trade Commission. <http://www.ftc.gov/news-events/media-resources/mergers-and-competition/pay-delay>.

214. "FTC Study Finds That in FY 2011, Pharmaceutical Industry Continued to Make Numerous Business Deals That Delay Consumers Access to Lower-Cost Generic Drugs." Federal Trade Commission. 25 Oct. 2011. <http://www.ftc.gov/news-events/press-releases/2011/10/ftc-study-finds-fy-2011-pharmaceutical-industry-continued-make>.

215. Id.

Chapter 8

216. Anderson, Stuart. "40 Percent of Fortune 500 Companies Founded by Immigrants or Their Children." *Forbes Magazine*. 19 June 2011. <http://www.forbes.com/sites/stuartanderson/2011/06/19/40-percent-of-fortune-500-companies-founded-by-immigrants-or-their-children/>.

217. "Infographic: STEM Skills Are Driving Innovation." Adecco USA. <http://www.adeccousa.com/employers/resources/Pages/infographic-stem-skills-are-driving-innovation.aspx>.

218. Id.

219. "A Guide to S.744: Understanding the 2013 Senate Immigration Bill." Immigration Policy Center, June 2013. <http://www.immigrationpolicy.org/

special-reports/guide-s744-understanding-2013-senate-immigration-bill>.

220. Bush, Jeb, and Clint Bolick. "A Republican Case for Immigration Reform." *The Wall Street Journal.* 30 June 2013. <http://www.wsj.com/news/articles/SB100014241278873243282045785716415 99272504>.

221. "Letter to New York Congressional Delegation." Partnership for a New American Economy, 19 Sept. 2013. <http://www.renewoureconomy.org/wp-content/uploads/2013/09/ny-letter.pdf>.

222. Zavodny, Madeline. "Immigration and American Jobs." American Enterprise Institute, 15 Dec. 2011. <http://www.aei.org/publication/immigration-and-american-jobs/>.

223. "America' S Prison Population: Who, What, Where and Why." *The Economist.* 14 Mar. 2014. <http://www.economist.com/blogs/democracyinamerica/2014/03/americas-prison-population>.

224. "World Prison Populations." *BBC News.* 20 June 2005. <http://news.bbc.co.uk/2/shared/spl/hi/uk/06/prisons/html/nn2page1.stm>.

225. "Gov. Cuomo's Bold Step on Prison Education." *The New York Times.* 18 Feb. 2014. <http://www.nytimes.com/2014/02/19/opinion/gov-cuomos-bold-step-on-prison-education.html>.

226. Liptak, Adam. "1 in 100 U.S. Adults Behind Bars, New Study Says." *The New York Times.* 27 Feb. 2008. <http://www.nytimes.com/2008/02/28/us/28cnd-prison.html>.

227. Petersilia, Joan. "What Works in Prisoner Reentry? Reviewing and Questioning the Evidence." *Federal*

Probation: A Journal of Correctional Philosophy and Practice. Volume 68 Number 2. <http://www.uscourts.gov/uscourts/FederalCourts/PPS/Fedprob/2004-09/whatworks.html>.

228. Lattimore, Pamela, and Christy Visher. "The Multi-State Evaluation of the Serious and Violent Offender Reentry Initiative." The Urban Institute, Dec. 2009. Web. <http://www.urban.org/uploadedpdf/412075_evaluation_svori.pdf>.

229. Davis, Lois M., Robert Bozick, Jennifer L. Steele, Jessica Saunders, and Jeremy Miles. "Evaluating the Effectiveness of Correctional Education: A Meta-Analysis of Programs That Provide Education to Incarcerated Adults." Bureau of Justice Assistance and RAND Corporation. 2013. <https://www.bja.gov/Publications/RAND_Correctional-Education-Meta-Analysis.pdf>.

230. Id.

231. Id.

232. Id.

233. Voorhees, Josh. "An Obvious Way to Help Keep Ex-Cons Out of Prison That Pays for Itself." *Slate.* 18 Sept. 2014. <http://www.slate.com/articles/news_and_politics/politics/2014/09/recidivism_and_mental_illness_iowa_s_central_pharmacy_pilot_project_is_an.html>.

Chapter 9

234. Bilmes, Linda J. "The Financial Legacy of Iraq and Afghanistan: How Wartime Spending Decisions Will Constrain Future National Security Budgets." HKS Faculty Research Working Paper Series RWP13-006, March 2013. <https://research.hks.

harvard.edu/publications/workingpapers/ citation.aspx?PubId=8956&type=WPN>.

235. Maffucci, Jackie. "Veteran Unemployment Rate Increases in July." Iraq and Afghanistan Veterans of America (IAVA). 1 Aug. 2014. <http://iava.org/ blogs/veteran-unemployment-rate-increases-in-july/>.

236. "Helping Veterans Start and Grow Small Businesses." Military.com and the United States Small Business Administration. 2012 <http:// www.military.com/veterans-day/helping-veterans-start-businesses.html>.

237. "Partnering with Your State Workforce Agency to Hire Veterans: Employer Success Strategies." Slide 19 16 Jan. 2013. <http://www.slideshare. net/DirectEmployers/8-partnering-with-your-swa-jan-15-2013>.

238. "Texas Veterans Leadership Program." Texas Workforce Commission. <http://www.twc.state. tx.us/tvlp/texas-veterans-leadership-program. html#service>.

239. Zoroya, Gregg. "Texas Program Links Veterans to Jobs." USA TODAY. 11 May 2012. <http://usatoday30. usatoday.com/news/military/story/2012-04-27/ texas-veterans-unemployment/54889194/1>.

240. Wilkinson, Tom. "Working to Match Area Veterans with Jobs." The Eagle. 9 July 2012. <http://www. theeagle.com/opinion/columnists/working-to-match-area-veterans-with-jobs/article_db5232c5-4a10-5cbb-8b7e-e365e7d96729.html>.

241. "Partnering with Your State Workforce Agency to Hire Veterans: Employer Success Strategies." Slides 42-46. 16 Jan. 2013. <http://www.slideshare.net/

DirectEmployers/8-partnering-with-your-swa-jan-15-2013>.

242. Phillip, Erica E., and Ben Kesling. "Number of Homeless Veterans in the U.S. Falls Over Past Four Years." *The Wall Street Journal*. 26 Aug. 2014. <http://online.wsj.com/articles/number-of-homeless-veterans-in-the-u-s-falls-over-past-four-years-1409089535>.

243. Id.

244. Thornton, Terrance. "New Philosophy Turns Tide for Homeless Phoenix Veterans." Independent Newsmedia Inc. 11 Dec. 2013. <http://arizona.newszap.com/northvalley/127891-114/new-philosophy-turns-tide-for-homeless-phoenix-veterans>.

245. Santos, Fernanda. "Program to End Homelessness Among Veterans Reaches a Milestone in Arizona." *The New York Times*. 15 Jan. 2014. <http://www.nytimes.com/2014/01/16/us/program-to-end-homelessness-among-veterans-hits-milestone-in-arizona.html>.

246. Keys, Scott. "Phoenix Becomes First City To End Chronic Homelessness Among Veterans." ThinkProgress.com. 23 Dec. 2013. <http://thinkprogress.org/economy/2013/12/23/3099911/phoenix-homeless/>.

247. Santos, Fernanda. "Program to End Homelessness Among Veterans Reaches a Milestone in Arizona." *The New York Times*. 15 Jan. 2014. <http://www.nytimes.com/2014/01/16/us/program-to-end-homelessness-among-veterans-hits-milestone-in-arizona.html>.

248. Id.

249. Wogan, J.B. "How Salt Lake City Solved Chronic Veteran Homelessness." Governing Magazine. 9 Dec. 2013. <http://www.governing.com/news/headlines/gov-how-salt-lake-city-licked-veteran-homelessness.html>.

250. Capra, Gina. "Veterans Health Administration Office of Rural Health Update." Department of Veterans Affairs. 28 May 2014. <http://www.nchv.org/images/uploads/Capra%20Rural%20Health%20Update%20May%202014%281%29.pdf>.

251. Id.

252. "Fact Sheet: The National Research Action Plan for Improving Access to Mental Health Services for Veterans, Service Members, and Military Families." WhiteHouse.gov. The White House. <http://www.whitehouse.gov/sites/default/files/uploads/nrap_fact_sheet_082013.pdf>.

253. Id.

Chapter 10

254. "Administration on Aging (AoA) Aging Statistics." U.S Department of Health and Human Services. <http://www.aoa.gov/Aging_Statistics/>.

255. "Elder Abuse and Neglect: In Search of Solutions." American Psychological Association. <http://www.apa.org/pi/aging/resources/guides/elder-abuse.pdf>.

256. "Research Brief: The Commonwealth's Official Source for Population and Economic Statistics." Penn State Data Center. Institute of State and Regional Affairs, 13 June 2013. <http://pasdc.hbg.

psu.edu/sdc/pasdc_files/researchbriefs/2012_
Detailed_County_Est.pdf>.

257. Statistics/Data. National Center on Elder Abuse.
U.S. Department of Health and Human Services.
<http://www.ncea.aoa.gov/Library/Data/>.

258. Id.

259. "Elder Justice Act Implementation." National
Adult Protective Services Association. <http://
www.napsa-now.org/policy-advocacy/eja-
implementation/>.

260. "Elder Justice Act, the Elder Abuse Victims Act of
2008, The School Safety Enhancements Act of 2007,
and the A Child Is Missing Alert and Recovery
Center Act." Government Printing Office. 17 Apr.
2008. <http://www.gpo.gov/fdsys/pkg/CHRG-
110hhrg41797/html/CHRG-110hhrg41797.htm>.

261. Colello, Kristen J. "The Elder Justice Act: Background
and Issues for Congress." Congressional Research
Service. 3 Sept. 2014. <http://fas.org/sgp/crs/
misc/R43707.pdf>.

262. Long-Term Care Services in the United States:
2013 Overview. Center for Disease Control. 2013.
<http://www.cdc.gov/nchs/data/nsltcp/long_
term_care_services_2013.pdf>.

263. "Genworth 2014 Cost of Care Survey." Genworth. 2014.
<https://www.genworth.com/dam/Americas/
US/PDFs/Consumer/corporate/130568_032514_
CostofCare_FINAL_nonsecure.pdf>.

264. "Table 5. Occupations with the Most Job Growth,
2012 and Projected 2022." U.S. Bureau of Labor
Statistics. <http://www.bls.gov/news.release/
ecopro.t05.htm>.

265. "America's Direct-Care Workforce." Phinational. Nov. 2013. <http://phinational.org/sites/phinational.org/files/phi-facts-3.pdf>.
266. Id.
267. "Genworth 2013 Cost of Care Survey." Genworth. 2013. <https://www.genworth.com/dam/Americas/US/PDFs/Consumer/corporate/131168_031813_Executive%20Summary.pdf>.
268. "America's Direct-Care Workforce." Phinational. Nov. 2013. <http://phinational.org/sites/phinational.org/files/phi-facts-3.pdf>.
269. "Commission on Long-Term Care: Report to Congress." Commission on Long Term Care. 30 Sept. 2013. <http://www.gpo.gov/fdsys/pkg/GPO-LTCCOMMISSION/pdf/GPO-LTCCOMMISSION.pdf>.
270. "Sestak Urges Congress to Pass Legislation Protecting Alzheimer Patients from Elder Abuse." Pottstown Newspaper. <http://pottstownherald.com/sestak-urges-congress-to-pass-legislation-protecting-alzheimer-patients-from-elder-abuse/1657/>
271. "Medicare Fraud Progress Made, but More Action Needed to Address Medicare Fraud, Waste, and Abuse. " Government Accountability Office. 30 Apr. 2014. <http://www.gao.gov/assets/670/662845.pdf>.
272. Abelson, Reed, and Eric Lichtblau. "Pervasive Medicare Fraud Proves Hard to Stop." *The New York Times*. 15 Aug. 2014. <http://www.nytimes.com/2014/08/16/business/uncovering-health-care-fraud-proves-elusive.html>.

273. Stewart, Christopher. "How Agents Hunt for Fraud in Trove of Medicare Data." *The Wall Street Journal*. 15 Aug. 2014. <http://online.wsj.com/articles/how-agents-hunt-for-fraud-in-trove-of-medicare-data-1408069802>.

274. Id.

275. "The Department of Health and Human Services and The Department of Justice Health Care Fraud and Abuse Control Program Annual Report for Fiscal Year 2012." U.S. Department of Health and Human Services. Feb. 2013. <http://oig.hhs.gov/publications/docs/hcfac/hcfacreport2012.pdf>.

276. Carlson, Joe. "HHS Inspector General's Funding Cuts Will Hurt Medicare, Medicaid Fraud Probes." Modern Healthcare. 26 July 2013. <http://www.modernhealthcare.com/article/20130726/NEWS/307269996#>.

277. "Social Security." Benefits Planner: Maximum Taxable Earnings (1937-2015)." <http://www.ssa.gov/planners/maxtax.htm>.

278. "The Evolution of Social Security's Taxable Maximum." U.S. Social Security Administration Office of Retirement and Disability Policy. Sept. 2011. <http://www.ssa.gov/policy/docs/policybriefs/pb2011-02.html>.

279. "Distributional Effects of Raising the Social Security Taxable Maximum." U.S. Social Security Administration Office of Retirement and Disability Policy. <http://www.ssa.gov/policy/docs/policybriefs/pb2009-01.html>.

280. "Social Security." Trustees Report Summary. U.S. Social Security Administration. <http://www.ssa.gov/oact/trsum/>.

281. "Contrary to "Entitlement Society" Rhetoric, Over Nine-Tenths of Entitlement Benefits Go to Elderly, Disabled, or Working Households." Center on Budget and Policy Priorities. 10 Feb. 2012. <http://www.cbpp.org/cms/?fa=view&id=3677>.
282. O'Keefe, Ed. "Millionaires Earn Billions in Federal Benefits, Report Says." *The Washington Post.* 14 Nov. 2011. <http://www.washingtonpost.com/blogs/federal-eye/post/millionaires-earn-billions-in-federal-benefits-report-says/2011/11/14/gIQAAjv6KN_blog.html>.

Chapter 11

283. Minutes of the Provincial Council of Pennsylvania: From the Organization to the Termination of the Proprietary Government. [Mar. 10, 1683-Sept. 27, 1775]. Vol. 1. J. Stevens. p. 532.
284. "PISA 2012 Results - OECD." Organisation for Economic Co-Operation and Development. N.p., 2012. <http://www.oecd.org/pisa/keyfindings/pisa-2012-results.htm>.
285. "Public High School Graduation Rates." National Center of Educational Statistics. Institute of Education Sciences, May 2014. <http://nces.ed.gov/programs/coe/indicator_coi.asp>.
286. Kurtzleben, Danielle. "CHARTS: Just How Fast Has College Tuition Grown?" U.S.News & World Report. 23 Oct. 2013. <http://www.usnews.com/news/articles/2013/10/23/charts-just-how-fast-has-college-tuition-grown>.
287. "Giving in Numbers." Committee for Encouraging Corporate Philanthropy. 2013. <http://cecp.

co/pdfs/giving_in_numbers/GIN2013_Web_
Final.pdf>.

288. McGinty, Jo Carven. "Test Scores Are No Sure Guide
to What Students Know." *The Wall Street Journal.*
11 Jan. 2014. <http://www.wsj.com/articles/test
-scores-are-no-sure-guide-to-what-students-
know-1405122823>.

289. Bennett, William. "The Conservative Case for
Common Core." *The Wall Street Journal.* 10 Sept.
2014. <http://www.wsj.com/articles/william-
j-bennett-the-conservative-case-for-common-
core-1410390435>.

290. "Frequently Asked Questions." Common
Core: State Standards Initiative. <http://
www.corestandards.org/about-the-standards/
frequently-asked-questions/>.

291. Torres, Alec. "The Ten Dumbest Common Core
Problems,." *National Review.* 20 Mar. 2014. <http://
www.nationalreview.com/article/373840/ten-
dumbest-common-core-problems-alec-torres>.

292. Davis, Michelle. "Adaptive Testing Evolves to Assess
Common-Core Skills." Education Week Digital
Directions. 15 Oct. 2012. <http://www.edweek.org/
dd/articles/2012/10/17/01adaptive.h06.html>.

293. Strohm, Chris. "FCC Approves $2 Billion
Boost for Wi-Fi in Schools." *Bloomberg.* 11 July
2014. <http://www.bloomberg.com/news/
articles/2014-07-11/fcc-approves-2-billion-boost-
for-wireless-internet-in-schools>.

294. Rockefeller, John D., and Edward J. Markey.
"Letter to The Honorable Thomas Wheeler."
United States Senate Committee on Commerce,
Science, and Transportation. 8 July 2014. <http://

www.commerce.senate.gov/public/?a=Files.
Serve&File_id=3526e03e-0c10-4e03-92c1-
4a93cf3f7fe5>.

295. Hunt, Thomas. "National Defense Education Act
(NDEA) | United States [1958]." Encyclopedia
Britannica Online. 15 Dec. 2015. <http://www.
britannica.com/EBchecked/topic/404717/
National-Defense-Education-Act-NDEA>.

296. Higher Education Tuition Increasing Faster than
Household Income and Public Colleges' Costs:
Report to Congressional Requesters. 1996. United
States General Accounting Office. <http://www.
gao.gov/assets/160/155555.pdf>.

297. Paulson, Amanda. "Student Debt: What's Been
Driving College Costs so High, Anyway?" *The
Christian Science Monitor*. 6 June 2014. <http://www.
csmonitor.com/USA/Education/2012/0606/
Student-debt-What-s-been-driving-college-costs-
so-high-anyway>.

298. "Student Debt at All-time High of $1.2 Trillion."
CNBC, 24 Sept. 2014. <http://www.cnbc.com/
id/102028451#>.

299. "FACTSHEET: Making Student Loans More
Affordable." WhiteHouse.gov. The Office of
the Vice President. 9 June 2014. <http://www.
whitehouse.gov/the-press-office/2014/06/09/
factsheet-making-student-loans-more-
affordable>.

300. Brown, Meta, and Sydnee Caldwell. "Liberty
Street Economics." Liberty Street Economics.
Liberty Street Economics, 17 Apr. 2013.
<http://libertystreeteconomics.newyorkfed.
org/2013/04/young-student-loan-borrowers-

retreat-from-housing-and-auto-markets.html#.
VDgm7PldXJZ>.

301. Id.

302. Ambrose, Brent W., Larry Cordell, and Shuwei Ma. "The Impact of Student Loan Debt on Small Business Formation." 31 Mar. 2014. <http:// papers.ssrn.com/sol3/papers.cfm?abstract_ id=2417676>.

303. Fry, Richard. "A Rising Share of Young Adults Live in Their Parents' Home." Pew Research Centers Social Demographic Trends Project RSS. N.p., 01 Aug. 2013. <http://www.pewsocialtrends. org/2013/08/01/a-rising-share-of-young-adults-live-in-their-parents-home/>.

304. Wang, Wendy, and Kim Parker. "Record Share of Americans Have Never Married." Pew Research Centers Social Demographic Trends Project RSS. 23 Sept. 2014. <http://www.pewsocialtrends. org/2014/09/24/record-share-of-americans-have-never-married/#gender-education-and-marriage>.

305. Chute, Eleanor. "Penn State & University of Pittsburgh Tuition Remains Highest." *Pittsburgh Post-Gazette*. 1 July 2014. <http://www.post-gazette.com/news/education/2014/07/01/Pitt-Penn-State-remain-highest-in-tuition-nationally-for-public-universities/stories/201406300178>.

306. "Interest Rates for New Direct Loans." Interest Rates for New Direct Loans. 2014. <https:// studentaid.ed.gov/about/announcements/ interest-rate>.

307. Berr, Jonathan. "Student Loan Interest Rates Rise, Worrying Some Experts." *CBS News*. 1

July 2014. <http://www.cbsnews.com/news/ student-loan-interest-rates-rise-worrying-some-experts/?wpisrc=nl_wonk>.

308. CBO's April 2014 Baseline Projections for the Student Loan Program. Congressional Budget Office. Apr. 2014. <http://www.cbo.gov/sites/ default/files/cbofiles/attachments/44198-2014-04-StudentLoan.pdf>.

309. Konczal, Mike. "The Devastating, Lifelong Consequences of Student Debt." 24 June 2010. <http://www.newrepublic.com/article/118354/ brookings-study-student-debt-misses-lifelong-consequences>.

310. "Subsidized and Unsubsidized Loans | Federal Student Aid." <https://studentaid.ed.gov/types/ loans/subsidized-unsubsidized>.

311. The Aspen Institute. "In Conversation with Stanley McChrystal." YouTube. 2 July 2012. <http:// www.youtube.com/watch?v=UzQBV4h1VtU>.

312. McChrystal, Stanley. "Lincoln's Call to Service — and Ours." *The Wall Street Journal*. 29 May 2013. <http://online.wsj.com/news/articles/SB100014 24127887324809804578511220613299186>.

313. Belfield, Clive. "The Economic Value of National Service." Aspen Institute. Aspen Institute, Sept. 2013. <http://www.aspeninstitute. org/sites/default/files/content/docs/pubs/ FranklinProject_EconomicValue_final.pdf>.

314. "A 21st Century National Service System: Plan of Action." Aspen Institute. June 2013. <http://www. aspeninstitute.org/sites/default/files/content/ docs/franklin/FranklinProject_PlanofAction_ final.pdf>.

Chapter 12

315. Aisch, Gregor, Joe Burgess, C. J. Chivers, Alicia Parlapiano, Sergio Peçanha, Archie Tse, Derek Watkins, and Karen Yourish. "How ISIS Works." *The New York Times*. 15 Sept. 2014. <http://www.nytimes.com/interactive/2014/09/16/world/middleeast/how-isis-works.html>.

316. Yan, Holly. "Why Is ISIS so Successful at Luring Westerners?." *CNN*. 7 Oct. 2014. <http://www.cnn.com/2014/10/07/world/isis-western-draw/>.

317. Orth, Maureen. "The Numbers Vladimir Putin Doesn't Want You to See." *Vanity Fair*. 31 Mar. 2014. <http://www.vanityfair.com/news/2014/03/numbers-vladimir-putin-doesnt-want-you-to-see>.

318. "NATO Accuses Russia over Ukraine." *BBC News*. 29 Aug. 2014. <http://www.bbc.com/news/world-europe-28984241>.

319. Alexander, Harriet. "Vladimir Putin Creating 'worst Human Rights Climate since Soviet Times'" *The Telegraph*. 24 Apr. 2013. <http://www.telegraph.co.uk/news/worldnews/vladimir-putin/10015065/Vladimir-Putin-creating-worst-human-rights-climate-since-Soviet-times.html>.

320. "Europe Needs an Alternative to Russian Natural Gas." *The Washington Post*. 5 Mar. 2015. <http://www.washingtonpost.com/opinions/europe-needs-an-alternative-to-russian-natural-gas/2014/03/05/31f30ac2-a321-11e3-a5fa-55f0c77bf39c_story.html>.

321. Mufson, Steven. "Oil Prices Are Falling - and That's Good for the U.S. and Bad for Russia."

The Washington Post. 2 Oct. 2014. <http://www.washingtonpost.com/blogs/wonkblog/wp/2014/10/02/oil-prices-are-falling-and-thats-good-for-the-u-s-and-bad-for-russia/>.

322. "Growth and Other Good Things." *The Economist.* 01 May 2013. <http://www.economist.com/blogs/baobab/2013/05/development-africa>.

323. Warner, Gregory. "Africa's Leaders Aim To Change Perception Of The Continent." *NPR.* 3 Aug. 2014. <http://www.npr.org/blogs/parallels/2014/08/03/337601447/africas-leaders-aim-to-change-perception-of-the-continent>.

324. Kulish, Nicholas. "Africans Open Fuller Wallets to the Future." *The New York Times.* 20 July 2014. <http://www.nytimes.com/2014/07/21/world/africa/economy-improves-as-middle-class-africans-open-wallets-to-the-future.html>.

325. Talev, Margaret. "Obama Building Africa Legacy by Changing U.S. Approach." *Bloomberg.* 4 Aug. 2014. <http://www.bloomberg.com/news/2014-08-03/obama-building-africa-legacy-by-changing-u-s-approach.html>.

326. "International Impacts & Adaptation." Environmental Protection Agency. <http://www.epa.gov/climatechange/impacts-adaptation/international.html>.

327. "The Expanding Middle." The Economist. 10 Nov. 2012. <http://www.economist.com/news/americas/21565930-decade-social-progress-has-created-bigger-middle-classbut-not-yet-middle-class>.

328. Barrientos, Armando. "Brazil: A Role Model for Development?" *The Guardian.* 17 Apr.

2014. <http://www.theguardian.com/global-development-professionals-network/2014/apr/17/brazil-role-model-development-africa>.

329. Campbell, Kurt, Nirav Patel, and Vikram Singh. "The Power of Balance: America in IAsia." Center for a New American Security. June 2008. <http://www.cnas.org/files/documents/publications/CampbellPatelSingh_iAsia_June08.pdf>.

330. "Secretary of Commerce Penny Pritzker Highlights Administration's Commitment to Asia-Pacific Region." United States Department of Commerce, 17 Apr. 2014. <http://www.commerce.gov/news/secretary-speeches/2014/04/17/secretary-commerce-penny-pritzker-highlights-administration%E2%80%99s-com>.

331. Id.

332. Id.

333. Rasmussen, Chris, and Elizabeth Schaefer. Jobs Supported by Export Destination 2013. International Trade Administration. 7 July 2014. <http://www.trade.gov/mas/ian/build/groups/public/@tg_ian/documents/webcontent/tg_ian_005372.pdf>.

334. Kirk, Ambassador Ron. "Trade Agreements Will Help Create Export-Supported Jobs in America." The White House. 04 Oct. 2011. <http://www.whitehouse.gov/blog/2011/10/04/trade-agreements-will-help-create-export-supported-jobs-america>.

335. Lowrey, Annie. "Obama Vow on Exports Is on Track, With Help." *The New York Times*. 20 Jan. 2012. <http://www.nytimes.com/2012/01/21/business/us-on-track-to-meet-goal-of-higher-exports.html>.

336. Greenert, Admiral Jonathan. "Sea Change: Navy Pivots to Asia." Foreign Policy. 14 Nov. 2012. <http://foreignpolicy.com/2012/11/14/sea-change/>.

337. Browne, Andrew. "Beijing Pays a Price for Assertiveness in South China Sea." *The Wall Street Journal.* <http://www.wsj.com/articles/SB10001424052702303627504579558913140862896>.; French, Howard W. "China's Dangerous Game." *The Atlantic.* 13 Oct. 2014. <http://www.theatlantic.com/magazine/archive/2014/11/chinas-dangerous-game/380789/>.

338. "The Report of The Commission on the Theft of American Intellectual Property." The IP Commission. May 2013. <http://www.ipcommission.org/report/ip_commission_report_052213.pdf>.

339. Fan, Ye. "US Firms Concerned by China Anti-Monopoly Crackdown." Voice of America. 11 Sept. 2014. <http://www.voanews.com/content/us-firms-concerned-by-china-anti-monopoly-crackdown/2447004.html>.; Dou, Eva. "Microphone Maker Knowles Faces Legal Challenge In China." *The Wall Street Journal.* 2 Apr. 2014. <http://blogs.wsj.com/digits/2014/04/02/microphone-maker-knowles-faces-legal-challenge-in-china/>.

340. Shiffman, John, and Andrea Shalal-Esa. "Exclusive: U.S. Waived Laws to Keep F-35 on Track with China-made Parts." *Reuters.* 03 Jan. 2014. <http://www.reuters.com/article/2014/01/03/us-lockheed-f-idUSBREA020VA20140103>.

341. Halper, Mark. "Weinberg Foundation: Sestak Pushes for Clean and Renewable Energy." Weinberg Foundation. 17 June 2013. <http://

joesestak.com/blog/weinberg-foundation-sestak-pushes-for-clean-and-renewable-energy>.

342. Id.
343. Bradsher, Keith. "Amid Tension, China Blocks Vital Exports to Japan." *The New York Times.* 22 Sept. 2010. <http://www.nytimes.com/2010/09/23/business/global/23rare.html?pagewanted=all>.
344. "FY 2013 Highlights." Export-Import Bank of the United States. <http://www.exim.gov/about/library/reports/annualreports/2013/highlights.html>.
345. Id.
346. Puzzanghera, Jim. "Lawrence Summers Goes to Bat for Endangered Export-Import Bank." *Los Angeles Times.* 7 July 2014. <http://www.latimes.com/business/money/la-fi-export-import-bank-summers-20140707-story.html>.
347. Quadrennial Defense Review 2014. The United States Department of Defense. 2014. <http://www.defense.gov/pubs/2014_Quadrennial_Defense_Review.pdf>.
348. Fears, Darryl. "Virginia Residents Oppose Preparations for Climate-related Sea-level Rise." *The Washington Post.* 17 Dec. 2011. <http://www.washingtonpost.com/national/health-science/virginia-residents-oppose-preparations-for-climate-related-sea-level-rise/2011/12/05/gIQAVRw40O_story.html>.

ABOUT THE AUTHOR

JOE SESTAK served in the Navy for 31 years rising to the rank of Vice Admiral, and then became the highest ranking military officer ever elected to Congress when he represented Pennsylvania's Seventh Congressional District for two terms. During his years in the service, Joe commanded an aircraft carrier battle group that conducted operations in Afghanistan and Iraq, served on President Clinton's National Security Council, and was the first Director of the Navy's anti-terrorism unit after 9/11.

In Congress, Joe was named the most productive member of his freshman class and had 10 pieces of legislation signed into law. In 2010, Sestak ran for U.S. Senate against the wishes of the entire Democratic Party leadership who were instead backing a 30-year incumbent that had switched from the Republican Party. Against an original 40 point polling deficit, Sestak won the primary but narrowly lost in the general by less than 2 percent after being outspent 3 to 1.

Sestak, who has a Ph.D. from Harvard, went on to teach courses at Carnegie Mellon University, Cheyney University, Dickinson College, Penn State Law, and the Army War College. He lives with his wife Susan and daughter Alex in Delaware County, Pennsylvania.

***

JAKE STERNBERGER earned his B.A. in Political Science with a certificate in Security Studies from Dickinson College, graduating *summa cum laude* and Phi Beta Kappa. He received his J.D. from Penn State Law. After Admiral Sestak gave a speech at Dickinson College in 2012, he asked Sternberger – then a student – how he thought the speech went. Sternberger told him that, frankly, it needed some work. Sestak has kept him around ever since.